The 20th Century's
MOST INFLUENTIAL
HISPANICS

Nancy Lopez
Golf Hall of Famer

by Anne Wallace Sharp

LUCENT BOOKS
A part of Gale, Cengage Learning

GALE
CENGAGE Learning

Detroit • New York • San Francisco • New Haven, Conn • Waterville, Maine • London

LIBRARY OF CONGRESS CATALOGING-IN-PUBLICATION DATA

Sharp, Anne Wallace.
  Nancy Lopez : Golf Hall of Famer / by Anne Wallace Sharp.
    p. cm. — (The twentieth century's most influential Hispanics)
  Includes bibliographical references and index.
  ISBN 978-1-4205-0060-8 (hardcover)
 1. Lopez, Nancy, 1957- 2. Golfers—United States—Biography. I. Title.
  GV964.L67S43 2008
   796.352092—dc22
[B]
                                                                                    2008010167

Lucent Books
27500 Drake Rd
Farmington Hills MI 48331

ISBN-13: 978-1-4205-0060-8
ISBN-10: 1-4205-0060-0

Printed in the United States of America
1 2 3 4 5 6 7 12 11 10 09 08

Table of Contents

Foreword

Hispanics in America and elsewhere have shed humble beginnings to soar to impressive and previously unreachable heights. In the twenty-first century, influential Hispanic figures can be found worldwide and in all fields of endeavor including science, politics, education, the arts, sports, religion and literature. Some accomplishments, like those of musician Carlos Santana or author Alisa Valdes-Rodriguez, have added a much-needed Hispanic voice to the artistic landscape. Others, such as revolutionary Che Guevara or labor leader Dolores Huerta, have spawned international social movements that have enriched the rights of all peoples.

But who exactly is Hispanic? When studying influential Hispanics, it is important to understand what the term actually means. Unlike strictly racial categories like "black" or "Asian," the term "Hispanic" joins a huge swath of people from different countries, religions, and races. The category was first used by the U.S. census bureau in 1980 and is used to refer to Spanish-speaking people of any race. Officially, it denotes a person whose ancestry either descends in whole or in part from the people of Spain or the various peoples of Spanish-speaking Latin America. Often the term "Hispanic" is used synonymously with the term "Latino," but the two actually have slightly different meanings. "Latino" refers only to people from the countries of Latin America, such as Argentina, Brazil, and Venezuela, whether they speak Spanish or Portuguese. Meanwhile, Hispanic refers to only Spanish-speaking peoples but from any Spanish-speaking country, such as Spain, Puerto Rico or Mexico.

In America, Hispanics are reaching new heights of cultural influence, buying power, and political clout. More than 35 million people identified themselves as Hispanic on the 2000 U.S. census, and there were estimated to be more than 41 million

Hispanics in America as of 2006. In the twenty-first century people of Hispanic origin have officially become the nation's largest ethnic minority, outnumbering blacks and Asians. Hispanics constitute about 13 percent of the nation's total population, and by 2050 their numbers are expected to rise to 102.6 million, at which point they would account for 24 percent of the total population. With growing numbers and expanding influence, Hispanic leaders, artists, politicians, and scientists in America and in other countries are commanding attention like never before.

These unique and fascinating stories are the subjects of *The Twentieth Century's Most Influential Hispanics* collection from Lucent Books. Each volume in the series critically examines the challenges, accomplishments, and legacy of influential Hispanic figures, many of whom, like Alberto Gonzales, sprang from modest beginnings to achieve groundbreaking goals. *The Twentieth Century's Most Influential Hispanics* offers vivid narrative, fully documented primary and secondary source quotes, a bibliography, thorough index, and mix of color and black and white photographs which enhance each volume and provide excellent starting points for research and discussion.

Introduction

LPGA Superstar

Twenty years before Tiger Woods became a superstar in men's golf, another young golfer took the golf world by storm. Her name is Nancy Lopez, and her rookie year on the Ladies Professional Golf Association (LPGA) Tour ranks among the greatest starts of all time. In 2002 sportswriter Len Ziehm of the *Chicago Sun-Times* described that beginning: "Tiger Woods may be the most influential player now, but Lopez's arrival in 1978 was much more explosive. In the first season on tour, Lopez won two tournaments early in the season, finished second in the next, and then won five in a row ... and she was only 21 years old."[1] Few athletes, before or since, have impacted a sport like the young Lopez did in her first year on the women's tour.

Like Tiger Woods, Lopez was a minority golfer whose father was a dominant figure in her golfing life. She began excelling at golf when she was a young child, and by the time she was twelve, she had won the New Mexico Women's Amateur. Lopez had also begun beating her father and other adult and junior players on a regular basis, just as Tiger would later do. And like Woods, she left college after her sophomore year to become a professional golfer.

Nancy Lopez began playing golf at a young age.

Unfortunately, also like Woods, Lopez struggled against racism and discrimination. There were not many golf courses open to Mexican Americans, much less a Mexican American woman. Her parents were denied membership in the Roswell Country Club simply because they were Hispanic. This prejudice against Hispanics was also evident in criticism about the way she played. "She was an intense competitor with extreme concentration before games. That attitude and the fact that she was a Mexican American winning so many tournaments did not sit well with others, but that didn't discourage her."[2]

Overcoming prejudice made Lopez a stronger person and probably a better golfer. Her husband, former major-league baseball player and manager, Ray Knight, once explained: "The pain that Nancy suffered as a young player, not being able to golf courses other people could play … certainly has molded her life."[3] And yet for all the prejudice and pain that Lopez experienced, she emerged stronger and more resilient. Her pleasing personality and extraordinary golf skills won over the fans, the public, and the sports world. She became a role model, not only for Mexican Americans, but for women around the world.

After an extraordinary rookie year, during which Lopez won nine events, she went on to have an illustrious career. In all, she won forty-eight tournaments, including three major ones: the LPGA Championship in 1978, 1979, and 1989. In 1987 she was the youngest woman, at age thirty, ever to be inducted into the LPGA Hall of Fame. In her acceptance speech, Lopez spoke of what an honor it was for her to be included with all the other great stars of women's golf.

Her fans, however, would tell Lopez that the honor was all theirs, in just being able to watch her play. She achieved greatness on the LPGA Tour through a combination of hard work and self-discipline. Yet, she never forgot her father's words that golf was supposed to be fun. She brought energy and charisma to the women's tour at a time when it was sorely needed. Her outgoing personality, along with her natural athletic abilities, helped make Lopez and the women's golf tour almost as popular as the men's tour. And, by always maintaining a cheerful and positive attitude, she endeared herself to millions of fans throughout the world.

Golf writer, Ron Sirak describes Lopez's appeal: "Long after the great shots are forgotten, long after the victories blur into an amalgam of images, Nancy Lopez will be remembered for one indelible thing. That smile. Oh, that smile."[4] Author Dick Wimmer agrees that her smile was part of Lopez's winning personality: "A beaming smile, a smile that rivals [basketball player] Magic Johnson's as the best in sports, a smile as warm as the sun, lit up her face after a great shot."[5] That smile and Lopez's friendliness and approachability made her one of the most popular golfers ever to tee up a golf ball.

In becoming so popular, she has been favorably compared to legendary golf superstar Arnold Palmer. Thousands of fans followed

Twenty year old Nancy Lopez showed signs of greatness from the start of her career. Here, she stands with fourteen year old tennis player Tracy Austin after being named LPGA Rookie of the Year in 1978.

Palmer around the golf course. Soon Lopez's galleries were just as large. She would often have to come to the golf course hours ahead of her tee time just to avoid the crush of those who followed her game.

Many golfers and sports analysts believe that Lopez could have become the greatest woman golfer ever if she had not set other priorities for her life. Despite her love for golf, she had other needs, as writer Paul Harber explains: "Her career has not soared to the heights that you might expect from a player with seemingly unlimited potential. ... Why? Lopez is enjoying a different challenge. Motherhood."[6] She made taking care of her daughters and spending time with her husband a higher priority than golf. Lopez tackled motherhood with the same enthusiasm that she had for golf. She has repeatedly stated that her family has been, and will always be, her first priority.

Despite not rising to the greatness that others expected of her, Nancy Lopez, nonetheless, has had a stellar career. In addition, part of her legacy is the immense impact she made on the game of women's golf. Eric Olson of the *Cincinnati Post* offers his opinion: "She was the face of women's golf for most of two decades and relishes her role as one of the game's great ambassadors."[7]

Chapter 1

A Golfing Prodigy

Nancy Marie Lopez was born January 6, 1957, in Torrence, California, but spent most of her childhood in Roswell, New Mexico. She was the younger of two daughters born to Domingo and Marina Lopez. Her sister Delma was twelve years Nancy's senior and, for much of Nancy's childhood, was married and living in California. As a result, Nancy was brought up pretty much as an only child, receiving unrivaled attention from both parents.

Nancy's father Domingo was born in Mexico but moved with his parents to Texas when he was just a boy. He eventually moved to Loving, New Mexico, where his family owned and worked on a cotton farm. Eventually, Domingo left home and ended up in Roswell, New Mexico, where he worked as a farm laborer. While living there, he met Marina, a Mexican American woman, whom he later married.

Domingo was a very athletic person and he was approached by a minor league baseball team to play for them. Concerned that he could not support his family on a baseball salary, he chose not to accept the offer. Instead, he enrolled in courses on automobile repair and eventually opened the East Second Body Shop. Marina did the accounting and raised the couple's two daughters.

Nancy was brought up in a very traditional and old-fashioned Mexican home. Typically, in such households, the woman is expected to stay home, raise the children, and see to her husband's needs, while the man works and provides financially for the family. Nancy carried many of these traditions into her own married life.

"The Significant Birth for Me"

When Nancy was eight years old, her mother got sick and was diagnosed with a serious lung disease. Marina's doctor recommended exercise and walking as the best way to overcome the problem. Domingo suggested golf as a form of exercise for his wife and the two began to play often. Because they couldn't afford a babysitter, they often took their young daughter Nancy with them to the Roswell, New Mexico, municipal or city course. To keep their daughter from getting bored, they would occasionally allow her to hit the ball. She amazed her parents almost from the first shot she hit.

Lopez explains what happened:

> "The significant birth for me ... took place on a fairway of the municipal golf course in Roswell, New Mexico when I was eight years old. My golf education began at the same moment ... Dad pulled Mom's 4-wood [a wood is a golf club used to hit the ball long distances] out of the bag, handed it to me, and simply said, 'Hit it. You just keep hitting it until you get that ball into the hole.' That was my first golf lesson."[8]

Nancy's parents were astounded when that first ball flew over their heads. Lopez continued to repeat the process as her parents finished their round. Lopez reports that from that moment on, she was totally captivated by golf. Her parents were so impressed with her early skills that they immediately committed themselves to her pursuit of the sport. Within six months, Nancy was a better golfer than her mother, who happily gave up her clubs so that Nancy could play with Domingo.

Her parents couldn't afford babysitters, so they often took Nancy to the Roswell, New Mexico municipal or city golf courses, where she first learned to hit a golf ball at age eight.

A Love Affair with Cars

Nancy Lopez has always had a love affair with cars. She obtained her driver's license when she was fifteen years old. Her parents then provided her with a brand-new canary yellow 1972 Gran Torino so that she could drive herself to out-of-town tournaments. She loved that car and soon got the nickname "Skeetch" from taking off quickly and screeching the tires. Her father eventually bought her another car—a Chevrolet Monte Carlo. When he gave Nancy the keys, he told her that the Monte Carlo was the last car he would buy for her. He knew in his heart that Nancy would succeed and be able to afford to purchase future vehicles.

After she began playing professional golf, Lopez often traveled to tournaments with her caddy, Roscoe Jones. She lessened the boredom of long drives by talking to others on the CB, or Citizen's Band Radio. She often told reporters how much fun it was to talk with others on the radio and how these conversations, not only kept her awake, but also kept her from being bored on long trips. Like other radio users, Lopez had her own special name or "handle." Hers was "Jive Cookie" because of her love of music of all kinds.

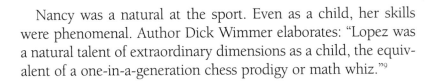

Nancy was a natural at the sport. Even as a child, her skills were phenomenal. Author Dick Wimmer elaborates: "Lopez was a natural talent of extraordinary dimensions as a child, the equivalent of a one-in-a-generation chess prodigy or math whiz."[9]

Financial Problems

From that time onward, Nancy played golf whenever she could. But, there were two obstacles in her way. The first one was money. The Lopez's only source of income was what Domingo made at the auto body shop; a sum that was barely enough to support them. The family lived in a two-bedroom, one-bath home with few luxuries. There was not much money left over for golf.

Realizing, however, that their daughter had exceptional talent, Domingo and Marina focused on providing Nancy with every opportunity to play golf that they could. Marina gave up golf in

Domingo Lopez (right), and Nancy, after Nancy won her 4th straight LPGA tournament in 1978. Domingo Lopez was the only golf instructor Nancy ever had.

order to save on green fees, and Domingo dug a big hole in the backyard and filled it with sand so his daughter could practice hitting golf balls out of a sand trap. Later, they also tried to put aside one hundred dollars a month so that Nancy could travel and play golf. According to Lopez, her father set up a budget and the rules were: "This money for Nancy's golf; this money for the house; this money for my job. In that order."[10]

Domingo, in particular, believed that Nancy could one day become a star. Writer Donna Adams explains: "He believed in his heart that his daughter would one day be famous, and he and his wife, Marina, scrimped and scraped together whatever they could to help their daughter succeed."[11]

A Famous Smile

"The family could barely afford orthodontic braces for Lopez but sacrificed so that she would have them. In Domingo's mind, the braces were important for someone who would one day be famous."

—Writer Lisette Hilton. Lisette Hilton, "Lopez Is LPGA's Knight in Shining Armor," ESPN.com. http://espn.go.com/classic/biography/s/Lopez_Nancy.html.

Nor could the Lopezes afford private golf lessons for their daughter. As a result, Nancy never had a formal golf lesson from a professional instructor. Domingo Lopez was the only golf teacher Lopez ever had. He was quite a good golfer and was more than capable of teaching his daughter the basics. He pretty much left Nancy's swing alone since, from the beginning, she could hit the ball long and straight. She learned by watching her father play and also by watching professional golfers on television. She would occasionally see things in their swings and then work on adding those touches to her own game. In addition, Lopez admits that she was born with an innate sense of what to do and how to play. The golf game came naturally to Lopez, and she required little advice from outside sources.

Lopez often wondered whether lessons would have helped or hindered her golf career. She had a very unconventional swing. Rather than a smooth tempo, she used a rather unorthodox way of swinging her golf club with a series of stops and starts. Later in her life, she had the opportunity to ask the great Mexican American golfer Lee Trevino what he thought about it. She noted that she had a bad swing and yet played quite well and successfully. Trevino responded: "You can't argue with success. If you swing badly but still score well and win, don't change a thing."[12]

Discrimination

For Lopez, playing golf was hindered not just by finances but also by prejudice and discrimination. Their hometown course, the Roswell Country Club, would not accept the Lopezes as members. Even if they had been able to afford the yearly fees, the country club refused to accept Mexican Americans.

Lopez later told reporters that, as a young child, she did not recognize the discrimination for what it was. It was only later that she realized the reason she could not play at the country club was because of racism and prejudice. Lopez comments: "All of us Lopezes are definitely … and unashamedly Mexican-American in Roswell, a town where that surely wasn't a social asset… We had the sort of minority status that minorities invariably suffer everywhere."[13]

As a result of not being able to play at the country club, Nancy was forced to play on the Roswell city course, a course that was not very well maintained or very challenging. The only virtue of the city course was that Lopez could play for a little over a dollar a round. In addition, the rough terrain and abundant sand hazards helped her learn how to play in adverse conditions.

Once her game improved, she was determined to enter amateur championships. (Young people often compete as amateurs; they receive no winning payment but gain valuable experience.) In order to enter these tournaments, however, Nancy needed to be sponsored by a country club. Despite her enormous talent, the Roswell Country Club refused to endorse or sponsor her. As a result, the Lopezes were forced to turn to a country club in Albuquerque, a city about forty miles from Roswell. This club readily accepted the Lopezes as honorary members and sponsored Nancy in her amateur events.

In addition to the prejudice on the golf course, Lopez also experienced discrimination from some of her friends. During her

The grounds of the Roswell Country Club are shown here in 2004. The Lopez family was not allowed to play the country club course because the club refused to admit Mexican-Americans at the time Nancy was learning the game.

childhood, most of Nancy's friends were Caucasian. While she admits to having good friends growing up, she also had some experiences where discrimination was apparent. The most glaring example is when she began dating a boy from her school. When his parents found out that Nancy was Mexican American, they forbade their son from seeing her again. "Today when someone tells me that certain old 'friends' from Roswell send me warm regards," Lopez wrote in 1979, "I sometimes have to take it with a grain of salt. A few of those old 'friends' don't raise tender memories."[14]

This kind of discrimination would follow Lopez throughout her life. In the late 1980s, she spoke of this prejudice:

> "Sometimes I'll go into a really nice shop, and the salespeople will either ignore me or hardly pay any attention to me. Then all of a sudden it will hit them that this isn't just another Mexican-American. This is Nancy Lopez, golfer and famous person. It's amazing to see their change in attitude... By that time, I'm out the door, because I believe strongly that people should be treated equally no matter who they are or what they do for a living."[15]

Winning

Despite the lack of money and the discrimination, Lopez found plenty of opportunities to play and improve her game. She entered her first tournament when she was nine years old, only a year after first being introduced to the game.

Her father had enrolled her in a Pee Wee golf tournament held in Alamogorda, New Mexico. The event was a three-day, twenty-seven-hole match for girls between the ages of eight and twelve. Nancy shot a sixty-two each day of the tournament and won by an astounding one hundred and ten shots! She was on her way to a career in golf.

Her father was so impressed and pleased that she had won her first tournament that he bought his daughter a special prize. Nancy was a big fan of Barbie dolls, so Domingo purchased a doll. As time passed, Nancy managed to gather quite a collection of dolls; each time she won an event, her father presented her with another doll. Lopez later told reporters that the dolls meant more to her than any cup or trophy at the time.

When she was ten, she won the New Mexico Girls' Championship by over sixty strokes and, by the age of eleven, was a better player than either of her parents. By that time, her father was determined

When she first started to enter tournaments, Lopez would receive a Barbie Doll from her father each time she won an event.

that Nancy should pursue the sport as a career. He was convinced that she was championship material. He encouraged her to enter every tournament they could find.

Before entering junior high school, Lopez won the Roswell City Championship. For this victory, the mayor of Roswell gave her free use of the city course she'd been playing on, as well as free use of another, and better, city course. When she was twelve, she won the New Mexico Women's Amateur Open, not the junior tournament

The Ins and Outs of Golf

Golf is a simple, yet complicated game. The game is generally played on an eighteen-hole course, with holes of varying distances. As a rule, there are four par five, four par three, and ten par four holes on each course, making for a total score of 72. In golf terminology, *par* is the score that players strive to obtain. Thus on an average hole, the golfer tries to get his or her ball in the hole with only four strokes. If the player uses only three shots on that hole, he or she has a birdie, and if the player uses five shots, then it's a bogey.

Each hole is comprised of several components. The tee box is where each player hits their first shot. The correct place to hit the shot is in the fairway, a mowed, grassy area that makes for an easy second shot. On either side of the fairway is the rough, where the grass is much higher, thus making the next shot much more difficult. The objective then shifts to trying to hit the ball on the green, an even more closely mowed area where the hole is. The player then uses a club called a putter (with a flat head) to hit the ball into the hole. Often sand traps or bunkers surround the green. These are referred to as hazards and are to be avoided at all costs as shots from these locations are often difficult.

A player can carry fourteen clubs in their golf bag. In addition to the putter, a player usually has four clubs called woods. These have big heads and are used to drive the ball off the tee box. They produce shots traveling the longest distance of any club in the golf bag. The remainder of the clubs are called irons; these clubs have heads that will produce shots of varying loft and are used to advance the ball from the fairway.

Nancy Lopez reacts as she barely misses a put at the U.S. Women's Open in 2000.

but the women's tournament. For that win, she received an armful of dolls from her father and mother. In winning this title, she shot a record seventy-five at the University South Course in Albuquerque, New Mexico. Her father said: "Nancy win. Nancy get every doll in the shop."[16]

Despite the heavy emphasis on golf during Lopez's early years, her parents also made sure that their daughter had a fairly normal childhood. Like other girls her age, she joined the Girl Scouts, took tap dancing lessons, tried gymnastics, and loved to swim. She also played volleyball, basketball, and touch football.

In addition to her activities, Lopez's mother made sure Nancy was prepared to become a wife. "Mom would take me shopping with her all the time and teach me the household things," Lopez reported. "If I didn't make my bed right, she'd often actually undo it and have me made it up again properly."[17] She was also required to do the normal chores and tasks that children often perform—with one exception. Her parents forbade their daughter to do the dishes. Domingo told his wife that Nancy's hands were made for golf, not doing dishes. He was afraid that the warm water would soften her hands too much.

High School Champion

After playing golf for several years and winning junior tournaments throughout the New Mexico, it was only natural that Nancy would want to continue golfing during high school. Unfortunately, Goddard High School did not have a girls' golf team. Lopez's solution to the problem was to play on the boys' team. But, the coaches at Goddard refused to let her try out for the boy's team because she was a girl. Her father threatened to contact an attorney and file a lawsuit. The board of education responded by formulating a new rule that allowed girls to play on the boys' team since a girls' team did not exist. Lopez became the only female member of the Goddard High School golf team.

Lopez repeatedly proved her merit by helping lead the Goddard golf team to the New Mexico State Championship in 1973 and 1974. She did this by playing according to the boy's rules. Usually, female golfers are allowed to tee their ball up in an area much closer to the green than the men's tees. Nancy,

Since there was no girl's team at her high school, Nancy became the only female member of the Goddard High School boy's golf team.

however, used the same tee areas that the boys did. Her ability to hit long shots off the tee made her one of the best golfers on the team. Even before graduating from high school, she could out-drive her opponents by at least fifty yards. (A drive is the first shot hit off the tee.)

During her high school years, Lopez also won the Western Women's Amateur Championship three times and the Mexican Amateur in 1975. In addition, she won the U.S. Girl's Junior Championship, the most important teen tournament in the United States, in 1972 and 1974. By the age of sixteen, her hard work and commitment to the game had paid off. Lopez had become the top-ranked women's amateur player in the United States.

Practice Makes Genius

"Her genius was honed through blindingly hard work."

—Author Dick Wimmer. Dick Wimmer, *The Women's Game: Great Champions in Women's Sports*. Short Hill, NJ: Burford, 2000, p. 65.

College Golf

After high school graduation, Nancy wanted to continue her education—and her golf—in college. During her senior year of high school, when it came time to choose a college, however, money again became an issue. Her parents simply could not afford the cost of a full university education. Out of respect for her parents and everything they had already done for her, Lopez refused to go further with her education unless she was able to obtain a scholarship to offset the expense of college. Her first choice of universities was Arizona State University, but that school did not offer golf scholarships to women, only men. She found similar problems elsewhere.

Ultimately, the University of Tulsa in Oklahoma agreed to give her a half scholarship to play on their golf team. While tempted to take the offer, Lopez knew that her parents still could not pay the remaining fees, and she told university officials that she needed a full scholarship. The university eventually agreed. Lopez became the first woman ever to receive a full golf scholarship to the University of Tulsa.

After being accepted at Tulsa, Lopez, still a senior in high school, entered the U.S. Women's Open, the most prestigious tournament in professional women's golf. Despite her youth, she played

extremely well and placed second. As an amateur, Lopez was not eligible for any of the prize money, but by finishing second, Lopez earned the Colgate Golf Scholarship, worth ten thousand dollars. This money would have enabled her to choose any college she wanted, but she decided to honor her commitment to Tulsa and enrolled there in the fall of 1975.

She planned to earn a degree in engineering because of her love of mathematics, but she found the course work extremely difficult. Compounding her problem was the golf schedule. The team was required to do an extensive amount of traveling and this resulted in team members missing numerous classes. "In a college where golf was important," Lopez reported, "I didn't get to learn much about engineering or calculus or chemistry."[18] She needed a private tutor her freshman year just to obtain a C average.

During her freshman year, she did well in tournaments and was named Tulsa's Female Athlete of the Year. She also won the prestigious Association of Intercollegiate Athletics for Women Championship. In the process, she earned solid All-American honors.

After a solid year on the golf course, Lopez returned home for the summer. When she arrived in Roswell, her parents noticed some changes in their daughter. Because of her academic struggles, Lopez had turned to food as a stress reliever. As a result, she had gained weight and it began to negatively affect her golf swing. With the help of her mother, Nancy tried to improve her eating habits, but her weight would continue to be a problem throughout her career.

When she returned to Tulsa in the fall to begin her sophomore year, Lopez was in good physical shape and had decided to change her major to business administration. She hoped that the courses would be easier to handle. And yet, the rigorous golf schedule once again negatively impacted her studies. Even with the tutor's help, Lopez's grades were barely acceptable and she continued to struggle academically.

She did not, however, struggle on the golf course. Lopez played extremely well, winning a total of eleven tournaments. Despite the fun she was having, Lopez yearned for more. In 1977 she realized that she was a better golfer than a student and made the decision to quit college and become a professional golfer. Lopez explains: "[College] competition was fine for awhile. But as I got older and better, I wasn't being challenged, and my game wasn't going anywhere. It was time to take my game to a higher level, the tour."[19] After the completion of her sophomore year, Lopez left the university and joined the ranks of professional women golfers.

Chapter 2

Rookie of the Year

By the time that Nancy Lopez became a professional golfer, women's golf had come a long way from its earliest years. Originally strictly an amateur game, women's golf had become more popular and was being played at a professional level. The difference in the two is a matter of money; amateurs receive no compensation for winning, while professionals earn prize money as well as endorsement fees.

By the 1940s, more and more women were interested in making a living playing golf. The first attempt to create a professional women's tour came in 1944 when the Women's Professional Golf Association (WPGA) was formed by several women golfers. The organization, however, barely survived five years. It was beset from the start by a lack of money and interest. The WPGA, however, did do two things that helped advance women's golf. It developed and started the U.S. Women's Open, a tournament that has endured to the present, and it led to the formation of the Ladies Professional Golf Association (LPGA) in 1950. According to the Web site History of Women's Golf in America: "Through perseverance and vision these followers of the 1st wave of women golfers succeeded, opening a new era for women's golf."[20]

Nancy Lopez became a professional in 1977 at a time when women's golf was still struggling. Women golfers were barely discussed on sports programs or written about in magazines of the time. The public still viewed female golfers as tomboys who were trying to play a men's game. The women's tour was in dire need of a female superstar to elevate the game to both prominence and respectability.

Nancy Lopez was just what the women's tour needed—a feminine figure with a giant swing and a smile so big that it captured the nation's heart. Her rookie year would become legendary and unrivaled in golfing history.

On Tour

When Lopez became a professional, there were perhaps one hundred women playing on the LPGA Tour. All of the women were members of the LPGA, an organization that governed the women's tour. Players were required to play in a certain number of tournaments, as well as win a predetermined amount of money. If a member failed to meet the requirements, she was not eligible to play on the tour. Golf, then as well as now, was a very competitive and tough way to earn a living. Lopez was determined to beat the many long odds.

Lopez soon learned that golf at the professional level was even more expensive than amateur golf. At the time, it cost nearly one thousand dollars a week to play on the tour. This price included transportation, hotel accommodations, food, and caddy fees. These expenses exerted tremendous pressure on the players to play well and earn tournament prize money.

Lopez was somewhat of a loner when she joined the tour, and she found relationships with the other players difficult to achieve. She later described the interactions with other players as being anywhere from friendly to jealous rivalry. She seldom went out with the other players, even to dinner, and usually roomed alone. She even found some of the players somewhat standoffish and cliquish, which only added to the loneliness and other pressures Lopez faced.

When Lopez turned professional, there were only about one hundred women playing on the LPGA Tour.

Tragedy and Victory

Despite the potential obstacles and challenges, Lopez was excited about joining the ranks of the professional players. In July 1977, she began her career by playing in three tournaments, finishing second in two of them. She was encouraged that she was playing well and making some money to offset the expenses.

In late September of that year, however, tragedy struck the Lopez family. Nancy's mother, Marina, had gone into the hospital for a routine appendectomy, but died before reaching the recovery room. Lopez and her father were heartbroken. Lopez temporarily quit playing golf following her mother's death and did not return to the game for nearly five months. She spent the time with her father, Domingo, grieving and trying to deal with the absence of her mother.

Lopez returned to the LPGA Tour in early 1978, announcing that she was dedicating the year to her mother. Shortly thereafter, she won her first professional tournament at the Bent Tree Classic in Sarasota, Florida. The tournament was a four-day, seventy-two-hole event. (Typically, women's tournaments are either fifty-four-hole or seventy-two-hole events. Eighteen holes are played each day.) Lopez shot a first round seventy-one and was two strokes behind Hollis Stacy. In the second round, Lopez repeated at seventy-one, while Stacy's score skyrocketed to seventy-eight. After the third round, Lopez and Donna White led several other players who were still within reach. On the final day, Lopez shot a seventy-three and won with a one-over-par score. She later told friends and reporters that from the moment she got the lead during the final round, she was determined to win.

It was a very emotional win for the young Lopez. She later told reporters: "I remember crying all the way down the 72nd fairway, knowing that I had the victory pretty well in hand unless I blew it completely, and I couldn't stop crying, right through the award ceremony, at which I dedicated my win to my mother's memory."[21] Lopez, to this day, says that this win was probably her most important and most meaningful on the LPGA Tour. She had felt her mother's presence watching over her and told reporters that this had toughened her mental game, enabling her to win.

For Lopez, her mother's death and her first win were turning points in her life. Lopez claimed that the tragedy of her mother's death had strengthened her both emotionally and mentally. She used this strength to improve her golf game; it also fueled her determination to win. This determination took the form of more aggressive play. During her first few events, she had played it safe. This was in keeping with the dominant feeling on the women's tour that players should not take risky shots but shoot instead for par.

Nancy Lopez stands near her mother Marina in 1960. Marina died
suddenly after a routine appendectomy in 1977.

Lopez's style changed after her mother's death as she began going
for birdies (one shot under par). Her aggressive style paid off.

In the week that followed her first victory, Lopez played in the
Sunstar Classic in Los Angeles, California. She won this tournament
as well. Suddenly people in the golf world were taking notice. For
winning in California, Lopez took home a prize of fifteen thousand
dollars. Even more important than the prize money, however, was
the fact that a number of magazines and newspapers began to cover
women's golf and write about Lopez's impressive victories.

According to Lopez, her next five tournaments were nothing
special. Her best finish was second place in the Kathyrn Crosby/
Hondo Civic Classic. Her next best round tied her for fifth place.
She continued to play well but did not win.

The Beginning of a Win Streak

Lopez then began a winning streak. She says in her book, *The Education of a Woman Golfer*, "I won the next five tournaments in a row, a feat unmatched in women's golf history."[22]

Her streak began in May 1978, when she won the Greater Baltimore Classic tournament at Pine Ridge Country Club in Lutherville, Maryland. She finished with a seven-under-par 210 to capture the title. This victory was followed the next week with another one at the Coca-Cola Classic at Forsgate Country

In 1978, Lopez won five LPGA tournaments in a row.

Club in Jamesburg, New Jersey, where she shot three under par to edge out her closest competition. An eleven under par at the Golden Lights Championship at the Wykagyl Country Club in New Rochelle, New York, made it three victories in a row for Lopez.

Winning a Big One

Lopez took the next week off in order to prepare for one of the major championships on the women's tour—the LPGA Championship. In 1978 the tournament was held at the Jack Nicklaus Golf Course in Kings Island, Ohio. The tough course, designed by golf superstar Nicklaus, was a challenge for all the competitors because of its well-placed sand traps, water hazards, and trees. The players were also challenged by the yardage – the course played much longer than the average course on the women's tour. The LPGA Championship was second only to the U.S. Women's Open in prestige.

Caddy Roscoe Jones

The man who caddied for Nancy Lopez during her triumphant rookie year was Roscoe Jones. Lopez met Jones through lawyer Bruce Lambon who, at the time, was caddying for her friend Jo Ann Washam. Lopez first worked with Jones at a tournament on Long Island in New York, where she finished second. Impressed with Jones's advice and easygoing personality, she hired him to be her permanent caddy.

Like Lopez, Jones is a very positive person. Lopez needed this kind of support and Jones supplied an extra degree of confidence. They worked as a team on the golf course. The two worked together in club selection, and he always encouraged her to believe in herself and her shot-making capabilities.

Lopez and Jones soon became the best of friends, traveling and often eating together while on tour. At one point, however, Jones became a little overbearing, trying to control her game, and she blew up at him and came close to firing him. She challenged him about the problem, and they were able to work things out. He continued to carry her bag throughout her first few years on tour.

Lopez's best round during the LPGA Championship came on the second day when she finished with a score of sixty-five. During a remarkable nine-hole stretch, she shot eagle, birdie, par, par, birdie, eagle, par, birdie, birdie. (Eagles are two-under-par scores.) She finished the next two days with scores of sixty-nine and seventy to capture the title with a thirteen-under-par score. Her score was six shots better than her closest competitor, Amy Alcott. With the win, Lopez moved into a tie with several other golfers, including legends Kathy Whitworth and Mickey Wright, who had won four tournaments in a row.

Setting a Record

From Ohio Lopez journeyed to Rochester, New York, for the Banker's Trust Classic, played at Locust Hill Country Club. By this time, the eyes of the sporting world were on the twenty-one-year-old player. Lopez told reporters that she was excited about the possibility of setting a new record in women's golf.

Lopez had become such a celebrity that she was asked to play in an exhibition match with entertainer and amateur golfer Bob Hope and former president Gerald R. Ford. Lopez later told reporters what a thrill it had been to play with two such famous people. Following this match, she drove to New York City where she was interviewed on the *Good Morning America* television program. She was asked to hit golf balls on the show, while singer Carly Simon sang one of her hit songs, "Nobody Does It Better." And it appeared as if no one, indeed, did it better than Lopez.

She started off well in the fifty-four-hole Rochester tournament, shooting a par seventy-two on the first day, but had a horrible experience on the second day that almost ruined the win streak. She hit an errant tee shot that bounded into the gallery of fans lining the fairway and hit a spectator on the head. Arriving at the scene, Lopez was sickened to see a man on the ground with blood on his head. She burst into tears. The man's name was Jerry Mesolella, a local dentist. He grimaced but said he was all right. "At least I'm going to get a chance to meet her,"[23] he said.

Lopez admitted after the round that had he been badly hurt, she would have dropped out of the tournament, win streak or no win streak. Fortunately, Mesolella had not been badly injured. Lopez pulled herself together after a bogey on that hole and ended the second day with a score of seventy-three. She recovered her poise, and on the final day shot a sixty-nine to win the tournament by two strokes.

She had done it—she had won five tournaments in a row. Lopez wrote about the victory and the streak: "Now I had really pulled it off! Five straight tournament wins for a new record, and starting right then, I guess I became a real, honest-to-goodness celebrity."[24] She smiled to herself as she recalled how her father had predicted that she would one day be a champion. During the five-tournament win streak, Lopez had an astounding score of thirty-nine under par. And she was only twenty-two years old.

Dealing with the Pressure

It was only after the five victories in a row that Lopez admitted to the immense pressure she had been fighting. "The pressure was there all of the time," Lopez said about the winning streak. "But it made me play better. It kept me on my toes. I really wasn't afraid of anything at that time."[25]

But she also admitted that it had been easier than she expected. "Golf was really easy during that five-in-a-row winning streak," she told one reporter. "The hole seemed big, the fairways seemed wide and I never hesitated. I just kept hitting it. … For those five weeks of golf, it just seemed really simple."[26]

Following her five victories, Lopez's life got even crazier as the pressure continued to increase. She was bombarded by people in the television industry and other media to make guest appearances. She appeared on *The Dinah Shore Show* and talked with the entertainer about golf. Shore herself was a talented golfer and a big promoter of women's golf. Lopez appeared on the cover of the *New York Times Magazine*, while *Time* and *Newsweek* also had articles about the emerging superstar. She reveled in the praise and attention she received, but remained committed to staying humble and never forgetting where she came from.

Accolades for her accomplishments came from everywhere, but the ones that mattered most to her came from her fellow golfers. One golf competitor, Judy Rankin, herself an excellent golfer

After her five tournament winning streak ended, Lopez admitted that there had been a lot of pressure to win, but it had also been easier than she expected.

and future sportscaster, called her "Wonder Woman" after the DC comic book of the same title. Thereafter, many of the newspaper and magazine reporters did the same. The "Wonder Woman" title came, in part, from her ability to hit long drives, nearly 275 yards off the tee. Her lengthy drives also earned her the nickname "Long Ball Lopez."

Wonder Woman

"She has the most poise and the most control of any young player I've ever seen."

—LPGA Hall of Fame female player Mickey Wright. Tom Callahan, "Golf's Wonder Woman," *Golf for Women*, November–December, 2002.

The long drives were impressive, but, according to sportswriter Doug Ferguson, what set her apart "was her knack for seizing the moment and scaring the daylights out of the front-runners. ... Her name on the leaderboard [a large outdoor board where the scores are posted] became an intimidating factor."[27] The golfing world now wanted to see Lopez win every week, an expectation that only increased the pressure on the young golfer.

Crowd Appeal

One of the factors that helped decrease the pressure somewhat was the public's warm support. During the five-tournament win streak, Lopez's gallery of fans grew in size and volume. The size of her galleries, in fact, was unheard of in women's sports. The fans responded warmly and vigorously to Lopez's smile, her winning ways, and her friendly personality. "I feel the vibrations from a crowd," Lopez said. "I feel them pulling for me."[28] She credited the strong fan support with helping her continue to play well. And she loved every moment of it: the crowds, the autographs, and the cheering. The fans' adoration helped ease the pressure Lopez felt.

Her fans started calling themselves "Nancy's Navy," a takeoff of "Arnie's Army," fans of golfer Arnold Palmer. Lopez loved the galleries and the fans returned that love. She claimed that the fans, rather

Lopez thrives on the support of golf fans, and has never shied away from signing autographs.

than distracting her, actually energized her. She loved to hear the cheers and encouragement the crowd gave her.

Lopez never shied away from signing autographs either, often signing as many as one hundred of them before a round and at least that many afterward. Lopez felt that giving her autograph was something she owed her loyal fans. She never lost sight of the fact that it was the fans who were helping to making her famous. Throughout her career, Lopez repaid them time and time again by making great shots, by signing autographs, and by talking to, and smiling at them.

In part, Lopez's attitude toward the fans came about because of an incident that happened when she was a teenager. She and her father had traveled to Los Angeles to watch a golf tournament that featured her favorite male golfer. At the end of the day's play, Lopez stood in a long line to get his autograph. When she finally got near the front of the line, he suddenly quit signing, muttering under his breath that he did not have any more time to waste.

Lopez was crushed, and despite her negative feelings about the incident, she has never identified the golfer. She has repeatedly talked about this incident and how much the golfer's attitude hurt and bothered her. She decided then and there that if she ever became a golf star, she would never refuse to sign an autograph. "I was only fifteen years old," she told one reporter, "and it made a big impression on me. I said 'Darn, if I ever turn professional, I am never going to make someone feel like he made [me] feel.'" [29]

Lopez also credited her father for helping her develop such a positive and outgoing attitude. "My dad was such a great inspiration to me," Lopez told one sportswriter. "He always told me to keep trying and never quit and always enjoy what I was doing. And always smile. If I can make somebody feel good by smiling at them or saying hi to them then I'm doing my job." [30] She, like other professional golfers, knew that the fans were an integral part of the game and that without their attendance, the tour would suffer. Because of the fans and their unwavering support, she became one of the few players on the tour who was also able to capture the attention of nongolfers. Her warm response to the fans helped advance the popularity of golf with the public.

In addition to the fans, she was also constantly surrounded by the media. Wherever she went, reporters wanted interviews or pictures. It did not matter whether she was winning or losing, the reporters were always present. Lopez loved every minute of it.

The Streak Ends

Despite the warm response and encouragement from the fans, Lopez's streak of victories stopped at five. It was in Hershey, Pennsylvania, at the Lady Keystone Open where Lopez's winning came to an end. Lopez was disappointed, but not really sorry. She admitted later that by the time she came to this tournament, she was completely exhausted by pressure of having to win each week. She told reporters that she had also lost her concentration. She finished the tournament in a tie for thirteenth place. Not winning was, in many ways, a relief for Lopez who could now take a breather and relax.

Nancy Lopez watches her shot during the final round of the Lady Keystone Open in 1978, where her five tournament winning streak came to an end.

After that loss, she finished off the year by winning two more tournaments, bringing her total wins in her rookie year up to nine, the most on the LPGA Tour since Kathy Whitworth won ten in 1966. Her final two victories were overseas. She won Europe's major women's event, the Colgate European Open, by three strokes. Lopez was thrilled to be back in the winner's circle and wrote about the victory: "It was a very prestigious and important title for me to capture and the perfect one in which to return to my winning ways."[31]

She then traveled to Asia where she competed in three events. In November 1978, she finished in a three-way tie for first in the Mizuno Ladies Classic, but lost in a playoff.

She then played in a mixed-doubles event with partner Ernesto Acosta, a well-known Mexican player; they won the event by three strokes but the victory did not count on the women's tour. Her final victory of the year came in the Far East Women's Invitation at Kuala Lumpur in Malaysia. She won by two strokes, bringing her earnings for the year up to nearly two hundred thousand dollars. This was more money than any rookie in golf history—male or female—had ever made. With the endorsements she was earning, her total winnings for the year exceeded four hundred thousand dollars.

Her Rookie Year

"Lopez ... exploded onto the golf scene ... at the age of 21, winning every tournament in sight and charming fans and sportswriters, who quickly dubbed her 'Nancy with the laughing face.'"

—Sportswriter Alice Steinbach. Alice Steinbach, "Nancy Lopez Knight: Golfer Extraordinaire, Mother, Wife Ordinaire," *Chicago-Sun Times*, May 17, 1987.

Her final statistics for her rookie year were impressive. She played in twenty-five events, winning nine and coming in second twice. Her average for the year was 71.76, while her score of thirteen under par at the LPGA Championship was the year's lowest and best score. No other player had won an event by such a low score. The year was also one for collecting trophies and awards.

Taking Care of Business

During her rookie year, Nancy Lopez met with Hughes Norton, a representative of Mark McCormack's International Management Group (IMG). At that time, the company was one of the few management groups that dealt primarily with athletes. The company's first client was legendary golfer Arnold Palmer; they soon added other big sports names, including golfers Jack Nicklaus and Gary Player, boxer Muhammad Ali, and tennis star Billie Jean King.

After meeting with Lopez's parents, IMG signed Lopez to a contract. Throughout the years that Lopez was with IMG, the company managed her earnings, furnished tax and legal advice, and arranged exposure and publicity for her. The company also got her television spots and arranged for her to be a contributing writer and editor for *Golf Digest*, the sport's primary publication. Lopez praised the company for taking so many details off her hands. She was also impressed that her agents had been able to double her tour winnings through careful investments.

The company also arranged endorsements for the up-and-coming star. Lopez signed a contract with the Florida Citrus Commission and promoted Florida orange juice. She also had close ties with Colgate and Palm Coast, a large development near Daytona Beach.

At the time Nancy Lopez signed a management deal with the International Management Group, the company also had other big-name stars, such as Arnold Palmer (right) and Jack Nicklaus, as clients.

Nancy Lopez won the Vare trophy, which is given for having the lowest scoring average on tour, in 1979.

She was named Rookie of the Year and Player of the Year on the LPGA Tour, as well as the Associated Press's Female Athlete of the Year. She also won the coveted Trophy, which is given for the lowest-scoring average on the tour. She remains the only woman ever to win Rookie of the Year, Player of the Year, and the Vare Trophy in a single season.

Accolades

Few rookies, before or since, have had such an illustrious first year in a sport. Sportswriter Bob Lutz may have summed it up best: "Women's golf had never seen anything like it: a Hispanic woman from a lower middle-class background dominating the women's tour as it had never been dominated before."[32]

Other sports reporters agreed. Alice Steinbach wrote: "The rest of the women on the pro golf tour can pack it in and turn to softball or roller derby for a living."[33] Randall Mell also praised her year:

"When she won nine times as a rookie, she lifted the women's game to a level of popularity it had never known."[34]

The women's game had sorely needed a superstar and Lopez readily became one. Inspired by Lopez, thousands of women across the country went out, bought golf clubs, and learned the game. Women's golf became much more popular largely because of Lopez. In addition, the size of the galleries increased dramatically in those tournaments that Lopez entered.

Lopez's peers were also abundant in their praise. Many of them were particularly impressed with how well Lopez had handled the pressure of not only being a rookie, but winning five tournaments in a row. Despite constant demands on her time, Lopez had just kept playing—and playing well.

With all these accolades flowing in, many people tended to forget Lopez's relative youth. Lopez, however, was very aware of her age and the expectations placed upon her. "Between traveling to tournaments, playing in them, honoring the commitments I had made for appearances and exhibitions, no day was long enough. … I wore myself out. … A girl needs some hours off to sleep, listen to records, wash her hair, watch television."[35]

In 1998 Lopez looked back on her winning season and commented: "You always remember the feeling. I just remember how exciting it was, the winning, and all the attention. It was a year I wish I could have every year."[36]

Chapter 3

Balancing Family and Career

Lopez had finished her rookie season in high spirits. She looked forward to another victorious year on tour, feeling confident that her success would continue. She felt particularly excited, however, because she had added a new dimension to her life. She had met someone, fallen in love, and was busily making plans for a wedding.

One of the things that Lopez had worried about when she became a professional in 1977 was the loneliness of being out on tour alone. While she had a close relationship with her caddy, Roscoe Jones, and had friendships with several of the women on tour, she spent the majority of her time by herself. She had earlier told her family and friends that she did not want to grow old playing golf and that she wanted to eventually marry and have a family. But she questioned whether the women's tour was a place where she could find a husband. The only men associated with the tour were either caddies or players' husbands. With her success and financial gain, she was also concerned about the possibility that a man might marry her for her money, not for love. When she met reporter Tim Melton, all her fears and concerns evaporated.

Endorsements

Nancy Lopez was one of the first female golfers to endorse and wear clothing made by a sporting goods company. Shortly after her superb rookie year, Lopez signed with FILA Clothing, an Italian apparel company that specialized in golf and tennis clothes. She was their first representative in golf. She found it exciting to wear such wonderful clothing and was even invited to design some of her own outfits.

Lopez favored wearing either long pants or a skirt when playing. She admitted that due to her weight she did not believe she had the figure to wear shorts. She also always wore jewelry when she played because it made her feel more feminine. She preferred bracelets and necklaces. In addition, she always wore bright colors when playing; they tended to enhance her dark black hair.

As a professional player, Lopez also received many gifts during her playing years. It was not unusual for automobile dealers to present her with a new car each year. These gifts and endorsement fees added income to the player's money earnings for the year.

Love at First Sight

During Lopez's five-tournament winning streak, some of her fellow golfers kidded her about her desire to meet someone and get married. She had laughed at their jokes and then put them out of her mind as she concentrated on winning. After her fifth victory, she journeyed to Hershey, Pennsylvania, for another tournament.

The week in Hershey was a hectic one for Lopez. She was constantly in front of the press being interviewed and photographed. She and her caddy, Roscoe Jones, had one interview with a handsome sportscaster named Tim Melton. For Lopez, it was almost love at first sight. After the interview, Lopez could not get Melton out of her mind. In fact, throughout the days of the tournament, she kept thinking about him to the point where it began to affect her concentration and even distract her playing.

Lopez soon confided to Jones that she thought Melton was very cute; she admitted that she would like to get to know him

Nancy Lopez appears with her caddy, Roscoe Jones. Jones played a role in bringing Lopez and sportscaster Tim Melton, her first husband, together.

better. In the meantime, Melton had noticed that Lopez seemed to be losing her concentration on important shots. At one point, Melton asked Jones why Lopez's game was off. Jones reported that she was quite fatigued but then suggested that Melton ask Lopez the questions personally. Soon thereafter, Melton called Lopez. They ended up having dinner together at an Italian restaurant. According to both parties, they enjoyed a good meal, talked for hours, and really connected.

Wedding Bells

After thoroughly enjoying each other's company over dinner, Lopez and Melton kept in touch by telephone for the duration of the Hershey tournament and then for days and weeks afterward. When Lopez played a few weeks later in Columbus, Ohio, Melton flew there to watch her play. After spending a few days together at the tournament, Melton invited Lopez to meet his parents, who lived in New Jersey.

Although Lopez and Melton originally intended to keep their engagement quiet, Lopez revealed the news of their upcoming marriage on the Today Show *in 1978.*

During the fall of 1978, Melton proposed to Lopez, and she accepted. They intended to keep the engagement quiet for awhile, but Lopez blurted the news out on the *Today Show*. Originally, they had set the wedding date for the spring of 1979, but the couple decided they did not want to wait that long. They were married on January 6, 1979, on Lopez's twenty-second birthday. Over one hundred and fifty people attended, including Jerry Mesolella, the dentist who Lopez had hit with her errant golf ball en route to her five victories. The couple married in a log cabin church called Cathedral in the Woods, set among the pine trees in Medford Lakes, New Jersey. After a reception, they flew to Hawaii for their honeymoon.

When they returned from their honeymoon, Lopez moved into Melton's apartment in Hershey, Pennsylvania. After lengthy discussions, the couple agreed that, at least for a while, Lopez's golf needed to come first before they started a family. Lopez explained: "The chemistry of my own makeup wouldn't let me slack off until I found out just how far I can go in this game I love so much."[37] She confided to Melton and her family that her goal was to maintain her number-one ranking. She still wanted to be the best golfer on the tour. Lopez later wrote: "I'm a very ambitious and determined woman about golf. I want to win every tournament I possibly can, and pile up a record that will give the ones who follow me something real tough to match or beat."[38] She remained totally committed to her career.

The Best Player on Tour

Lopez's determination to be the best player on the tour resulted in a great year. She won eight tournaments out of the twenty-two she entered. Her victories in this second year on tour brought her total wins as a professional up to seventeen, and she was still only twenty-three years old.

At the end of 1979, she was again named Professional Golfer of the Year and also earned her second Vare Trophy. During those two years, Nancy Lopez not only dominated the tour but also had become the most popular player on the LPGA tour.

During the early 1980s, Lopez continued to surpass many of her fellow golfers, winning three times each in 1981 and 1982.

She and Melton spent what time they could together, but their jobs kept them apart for weeks at a time. Lopez was usually out on the women's tour, and because of his job, Melton could not always travel with her. The strain of being separated for such long periods soon began to negatively affect their marriage.

The Player to Watch

"Nancy is the most compelling player on the LPGA Tour."

—Author Don Wade. Nancy Lopez and Don Wade, *The Complete Golfer*. Chicago, IL: Contemporary, 1987, p. ix.

Lopez felt guilty about being away so often, while at the same time, she resented that Melton pressured her to be home. Soon, Lopez's golf game suffered. She also began to eat to help ease her feelings of frustration; her weight blossomed and her game deteriorated. Suddenly, she could not play the kind of golf she was used to playing. She slid from number one on the money list, a compilation of each player's earnings on the tour, to number seven. Eventually, after emotionally draining arguments and long discussions, the couple agreed on a separation. Lopez later told reporters that they had just grown apart.

Ray Knight

Lopez turned to an old friend for support during this stressful time in her life. That friend was baseball player Ray Knight, a man who she and Melton had first met during her Asian tour at the end of her rookie year. Lopez describes how the relationship developed:

> I was playing in a tournament there and Ray was on a goodwill tour (with the Cincinnati Reds). ... I was engaged to be married. Then I got married and moved to Cincinnati. And Ray was there. Ray and Tim became good friends, and during that time Ray went through his divorce and my husband got a job in Houston.[39]

Lopez turned to her friend, Major League Baseball player Ray Knight, when the problems in her own marriage intensified.

Not long afterward, Knight was traded to the Houston Astros, and he moved into the same neighborhood where Melton and Lopez lived. Ray's own marriage had ended in a divorce and it seemed only natural that he would discuss his problems and feelings with the Meltons.

Because of the Knight's own struggle in his marriage, Lopez turned to him when the problems in her own marriage intensified. She told reporter Alice Steinbach that "[Ray] kept encouraging me to work it out, and during that time we became good friends. … He really supported me during that time."[40] Despite her efforts to save the marriage, however, Lopez eventually divorced Melton. She told Knight and other friends that she felt like a failure.

Ray Knight

Charles Ray Knight, born in 1952, married Nancy Lopez in 1982. During the early years of their marriage, both were busy with their own careers. Ray was a right-handed baseball player during the 1970s and 1980s. He made his major-league debut with the Cincinnati Reds in 1974, playing third base. He was an All-Star with that team in 1980 before being traded to the Houston Astros. He also played with the New York Mets, Baltimore Orioles, and Detroit Tigers.

Knight is perhaps best remembered for his play in the 1986 World Series. Playing for the New York Mets, he scored the winning run in the sixth game, only to follow that with a tie-breaking home run in game seven that won the series for the Mets. For his contributions, he won the Most Valuable Player Award for the 1986 World Series. He also won the Babe Ruth Award for the National League as well as the Sporting News Comeback Player of the Year.

Later traded to the Orioles and Tigers, Ray completed his career with a .271 batting average, a total of 84 homeruns, and 595 runs batted in. His baseball career then turned to managing the Cincinnati Reds from 1996 to 1997 and for one game in 2003. His record as a manager was 125–137.

Since his retirement from baseball, he has caddied for his wife, worked as an analyst for ESPN, and served as the postgame sports analyst for the Washington Nationals baseball team.

Golfer Nancy Lopez and her family celebrate her induction into the LPGA Hall of Fame in 1987.

Remarriage

After her divorce was finalized, Lopez's friendship with Knight turned into a romantic relationship. After dating for five months, they married in October 1982 and moved to Ray's hometown of Albany, Georgia. There, Lopez was welcomed into the extended Knight family of parents, sisters, nieces, and nephews.

Lopez later explained that her marriage to Ray Knight gave her an extra boost in her career, in her personal life, and most importantly, in her peace of mind. "I'm so happy with my life," she stated. "Now when I play, there is no pressure. It's just all fun, and when it's fun, you perform better."[41] Her happiness at home seemed to only enhance her career.

While his schedule in baseball and hers in golf did not give them much time together, Lopez reported that the marriage was sound. "I think that if you're married to somebody in a sport, they understand your ups and downs and can relate to what you're feeling."[42] The two made every attempt to be together and to support one another as they tried to balance two very busy schedules. In spite of those attempts, however, Lopez was able to catch only an occasional baseball game, and Ray managed to attend about one golf event per year.

Balancing Home and Career

Despite the busy schedules and the time they spent apart, Knight was very supportive of his wife's golf career and encouraged her to keep playing. Lopez, however, cut back her schedule to spend as much time as she could with her husband. She said simply that Knight made her happier than golf did. One year after marrying, Lopez gave birth to the couple's first child, Ashley Marie, in 1983. She played little golf that year and was content to stay home. Even as a nearly full-time mother, Lopez still managed to win two tournaments that year. Her winnings in those events enabled her to surpass the million-dollar mark in earnings.

Lopez found herself balancing her desire to be home with her family and her sports career. While her love of golf remained strong, her family became her first priority. "All the glamour, fame, signing autographs, and admiration doesn't mean anything if you

Lopez gets a hug from her 20-month-old daughter, Ashley Marie, in 1985.

don't have anything at home. We have a lot of love in our family."[43] She also found that the happiness she felt with Knight and her daughter helped her golf game. She was, as her father told her numerous times as a child, "playing happy."

And yet, during those times when she was out on tour without either Knight or her daughter, she yearned to be home. She admits that those feelings for home affected her play. Lopez, nonetheless, managed to win twenty times, although her winning percentage dropped. Before the birth of her first daughter, Lopez had won an amazing 27 out of the 131 tournaments she entered, a stunning 20 percent. After her first daughter was born, however, she won only 21 of 257, or 8 percent.

Despite her failure to recapture the glory of her first two years, Lopez remained a very competitive golfer. The fact that she was able to balance her priorities amazed many of her fellow competitors. Her caddy in the 1980s was Dan Wilson. He spoke of Lopez's ability to balance home and career: "She's the easiest player I ever worked for. It's amazing. When she's out here, she has the ability to solely focus on golf. Then she goes home and does all that other stuff."[44]

The Eighties

With Knight's support and encouragement, Lopez played in a number of tournaments in 1984, with her daughter Ashley and a nanny accompanying her. She won two tournaments that year. While not as active on the tour as she had once been, Lopez still managed to win at least once a year from 1985 until 1992, with the exception of one year. She also won at least one tournament during two of three years she gave birth. During those years, she played until she was five months pregnant. Despite her frequent absences from the tour, Lopez continued to be the player to beat.

A Performance to Remember

"One of the most dominating sports performances in half a century."

—Bruce Norman of *Sports Illustrated*. "Nancy Lopez Biography," BookRags Web site. www.bookrags.com/Nancy_Lopez.

Her best year since her eight victories in 1979 was 1985. Lopez won five tournaments, including the prestigious major event, the LPGA Championship, which she won by an impressive eight-stroke margin. She claimed 416,000 dollars in prize money. The year 1985 was also important because Lopez became the first woman to reach a score of twenty under par. She accomplished this by making twenty-five birdies during the Henredon Classic. She also led the money list that year and took home Player of the Year honors for the third time in her career. She led the tour in scoring with an average of 70.73, her best year by far since her eight victories in 1979, and captured the Vare Trophy for the third time. She repeated as Player of the Year in 1988.

In 1987, Nancy Lopez became the youngest player ever inducted into the LPGA Hall of Fame.

She played in, but did not win, four events in 1986, the year her second daughter, Erinn, was born. Although she only entered four tournaments, she finished in the top five in three of them. Despite her strong finishes, many sports analysts questioned whether Lopez's family was putting an undue strain on her golf. "She doesn't support that theory," wrote sportswriter Sally Jenkins. "Although Lopez rarely practices at home, she will spend all day at the course while on tour, and still plan dinner with the children every night, which she says relaxes her. She admits once Ashley reaches school age in another two years, she will cut her schedule to the bare minimum of majors and some warm-up tournaments."[45]

Lopez often traveled with her children along with a nanny to care for them while she practiced and played. Lopez spoke of having the girls with her to Jenkins: "I like them here with me. I wouldn't like having them at home. It relaxes me. ... I won't leave them at home for more than a week at a time."[46]

"She Has Staying Power"

The year 1987 was a somewhat inconsistent one for Lopez on tour. She did win at Sarasota but then slid to a thirty-ninth-place finish in her next tournament. After other low finishes, she took a month off to be with her family and regroup. When she returned, she managed a tie for second in Virginia, moving her up to seventeenth on the money list for the year.

Also in 1987, Lopez was inducted into the LPGA Hall of Fame. At thirty years old, she was the youngest player to ever earn the honor. At that time, it was extremely difficult to gain entry into the Hall of Fame because of several stringent requirements. A player had to have won at least thirty tournaments, along with at least two major events. Lopez had already managed to fulfill these obligations.

In a moving ceremony, Lopez told the audience: "I feel honored to be with the other women in the Hall of Fame. I have always respected them and what they have done for women's golf."[47] Lopez was also named the Golfer of the Decade by *Golf Magazine*, and she would later be named to the World Golf Hall of Fame.

By the end of 1987, Lopez had also passed the 2-million-dollar mark in golf and golf-related earnings. Sportswriters continued to

After her election to the LPGA Hall of Fame, Lopez was also named the Golfer of the Decade by Golf *Magazine.*

praise her game and her importance to the women's tour. Author Don Wade wrote in 1987:

> Over the past ten years, Nancy has proven that she has staying power. Even after reducing her playing schedule, she's still the player to watch. Anyone who doubts that need only ask the fans, the tournament sponsors, LPGA officials, or network television executives.[48]

In addition to her other commitments, Lopez also made the time to cowrite a book with Don Wade. *The Complete Golfer*, published in 1987, includes tips to women golfers just starting out. Lopez also summarizes her career and her priorities: "I've learned a lot about setting priorities—my family, my golf, myself—and the need to find a comfortable center to balance all the demands on my time and my feelings. ... As important as my golf is to me, my family is more important."[49] She repeatedly told reporters that it was her family that provided stability in her very hectic and demanding schedule.

Wade summarizes: "Like all great champions, she has a remarkable ability to concentrate fully on the job at hand, whether it's playing with the kids, being a wife to Ray, practicing putting, or giving yet another in a seemingly endless series of interviews."[50] Lopez had thus far proved very adept at balancing her golf career with her priorities at home.

Chapter 4

Struggling to Find Her Game

As Lopez entered the 1990s, she continued to balance her priorities between her family and her golf career. Cutting back on her golf schedule somewhat, she remained committed to making her family her number-one priority. The birth of a third daughter, Torri Heather in 1991, further curtailed her time on the tour. Lopez remained a strong figure on the women's tour even though her golf time was limited. Playing in only a dozen or so tournaments a year, she still managed to finish fourteenth, twenty-fifth, and twenty-eighth on the tour's money list in 1993, 1994, and 1995. She readily admitted, however, that her game had deteriorated. Not satisfied with her play, during the latter half of the 1990s, she committed herself to improving her health and her golf game in an effort to regain her earlier form and success.

Recapturing the Spark

Despite her fierce determination to play well, Lopez struggled during most of the 1990s to recapture the spark that had led to so many wins early in her career. She continued to find it difficult

In the 1990s, with competition on the women's tour improving so dramatically, young stars like Annika Sorenstam (pictured) began to make a name for themselves on tour and with the public.

to balance tournament golf with her family responsibilities. She played a limited amount on the tour simply because she wanted to spend time with her children and husband.

From 1991 when her third daughter Torri was born onward, Lopez played sporadically and erratically. Victories were few and far between, in part because of her limited play, but also because the competition on the women's tour had improved so dramatically. Players like Karrie Webb, Laura Davies, and Juli Inkster were winning with regularity and many other young stars, including Annika Sorenstam, were beginning their careers. Lopez states: "When I started, there were maybe ten players who could win. You could almost pick the winner every week. Now I would say the top thirty-five players could win on any given week."[51]

Rededicating Her Game

In 1995 realizing that she was not competitive enough to win anymore, Lopez decided to focus more intensely on her game. It had been over three years since she had last won a tournament. She announced her decision to reporters early in the year: "I'm rededicating myself to the game this year. I haven't done justice to myself over the past two years."[52] Reporter Bob Harig elaborated on her decision: "If she were to be anything more than a ceremonial golfer, if she wanted to compete as she did in the old days and try to win tournaments, Lopez needed to make a change."[53]

The biggest change Lopez had to make was getting back in shape. Her weight had blossomed once again and she knew she needed to commit herself to drastically dropping the extra pounds. Lopez had struggled with her weight since her college days. A lover of junk and snack foods, Lopez had readily admitted over the years to being what she laughingly referred to as "fat."

In 1996 when she was thirty-nine years old, Lopez decided yet again to do something about her weight. She told reporters:

> When I turned 39 it really bothered me. ... I'm about fifty pounds overweight. I don't feel good. I feel tired. I either really need to quit playing golf and go home or do something that is going to make me feel better

about my golf game and about myself. ... I'm either going to lose weight, get in shape, and start playing well, or I'm going to go home and quit playing golf.[54]

To accomplish her goal, Lopez hired a personal trainer who oversaw a strict diet and exercise regimen. This included work on a treadmill and stationary bicycle, along with two-hour exercise workouts six days a week. Lopez also began eating fruit and vegetables instead of the Big Macs, Doritos, and pizza she adored. As she lost pound after pound, she began to realize she had more energy. With the energy came an improvement in her golf game. After several months on the new regimen, she admitted that she was feeling much stronger and more confident. She spoke in particular of the improvement in her physical endurance during a long, four-day tournament.

Lopez's hard work began to pay off later that same year when she finished third in the Nabisco Dinah Shore Tournament. In addition, she led the second round of the LPGA Championship, although she ended up finishing third. And in August, she finished second in the Du Maurier Classic, finishing out the year with several top-twenty finishes. She also managed to finish the 1996 season by placing twentieth on the money list. Her golf game had improved and her weight loss and conditioning were paying off. Despite the improvement, Lopez was still hoping for better. She wanted another victory.

Another Win

The victory the Lopez wanted came in 1997; a year that saw Lopez returning to her old championship form. She proved that year that she was not washed out or ready for retirement. Her long sought-after win came at the Chick-Fil-A Charity Championship in April. Torrential rain led to the last two rounds being cancelled but Lopez, who was ahead after the first thirty-six holes, had her victory—the forty-eighth of her illustrious career.

She followed that victory with a sixth-place finish in a Daytona Beach tournament. After the tournament, she told reporters that her diet and exercise regimen had helped her overcome the extreme tiredness she had felt for so long. She also stated that she was encouraged that she was playing better than she had in many years.

Lopez was ecstatic about her play. The LPGA was thrilled as well to have one of its most famous competitors back on the course and playing well. "One of the things I absolutely love about our tour right now is how we have Hall of Famers who are not here for show," said Jim Ritts, LPGA commissioner. "I was thrilled to see Nancy Lopez win."[55]

Nancy Lopez plays golf at the LPGA Chick-Fil-A Charity Championship in April 1997. She won the tournament, which was her first win since 1993.

The LPGA

Women have been playing golf for hundreds of years. As author Jack Canfield explains: "Women have been a part of the game of golf since its earliest days. From Mary, Queen of Scots, to today's current crop of young, exciting athletes, the game has come a long way since the days of flowing Victorian-era dresses and hickory-shafted golf clubs."[1]

Part of that growth has been as a result of the development of the professional game through the auspices of the Ladies Professional Golf Association, or LPGA. This organization originated in 1950 with eleven tournaments and a total purse of forty-five thousand dollars. By the mid-1990s, the tour had grown to nearly forty events with a total purse of over 26 million dollars. Women's golf, however, has not always been popular. As author Steve Lynas explains: "The history of women's golf has been one of constant struggle. Women were neither liked for taking up the game, nor welcome in the clubhouse. Few people either expected, or wanted, them to do well."[2] Despite many obstacles, however, the LPGA has been successful and has paved the way for female athletes to compete for purses that today number in the millions of dollars.

1. Jack Canfield et al., *Chicken Soup for the Woman Golfer's Soul*. Deerfield Beach, FL: Health Communications, 2007, p. xv.
2. Steve Lynas, *The Complete Book of Golf*. London: Andre Deutsch, 1997, p. 117.

The U.S. Women's Open

Despite her forty-eight wins, Lopez told reporters that there was one glaring hole in her accomplishments. She wanted to win the U.S. Women's Open, an event she had long yearned to add to her list of victories. The Open was one of the most coveted titles in women's golf. Sportswriter Gary D'Amato elaborates: "Only a fool would suggest her career is incomplete, but what matters is what Lopez thinks. And more than anything else, she wants to win the Open. Yearns to win it. Burns to win it."[56]

Lopez had come close on several occasions. She came in second while still in high school and again two additional times. In 1997 at the age of forty and near the end of her long career, she arrived at Pumpkin Ridge Golf Club in Portland, Oregon, believing that she might have a chance. She had been working on her game, lost weight, and was in the best shape she had been in years. "It's been a long, long time," she told reporters, "since I've looked forward to coming to the course this much."[57]

After an interview with Lopez, sports reporter Jason Vonders summed up her attitude entering the tournament: "A 40-year-old mother of three … Lopez has been seeking rebirth in her golf game. She has lost forty pounds from exercise and diet in the last year and searched for the right mental attitude toward the only tournament she needs to win."[58] Going into the event, Lopez reported that she felt calm and excited to be playing good golf again. She also reported that she had more energy than she had had in years. She believed she had a good chance of winning.

Playing Like a Champion

Lopez played the course at Pumpkin Ridge like the champion she is and always has been. After three rounds in the sixties, she was in contention for the tournament she had always wanted to win. The excitement could be felt all over the course. Reporters and television cameras followed her every move, while Lopez's fans walked the course with her, cheering her every shot.

In the final round, fellow competitor Alison Nicholas had a four-shot lead over Lopez with only six holes to play. Lopez closed to within one stroke going into the eighteenth hole. She burst into tears, however, when her fifteen-foot birdie putt missed on the eighteenth hole—a birdie that would have tied her for the lead and resulted in a playoff. The putt slid by the hole by only an inch.

An Honor

"It's amazing now that I've played with her today. It's just a sheer privilege. I'll remember it for the rest of my life."

—Golfer Alison Nicholas, after playing with Lopez in the 1997 U.S. Women's Open. Jason Vonders, "Nancy Lopez, She's Anything but a Loser," *Columbian*, July 15, 1997.

Many of her fellow competitors had also been hoping to see Lopez win. Kim Williams, one of the golfers, said: "I played in the

Nancy Lopez chips at the second hole during the final round of the U.S. Women's Open at the Pumpkin Ridge Golf Club in 1997.

second-to-last group in front of Lopez. It was a great experience to see such an outpouring of support for her. It was amazing. There were 35,000 people praying for her to make that putt on 18."[59] Jan Stephenson, another golfer, said much the same thing, telling reporters that many of the players were pulling for Lopez to win as well.

Sportswriter Lew Price elaborated on the finish:

> At 40, desperately seeking the missing title she most covets, Lopez needed only to hole one final birdie putt to force a playoff ... and have a chance to complete what would have been the most fanciful victory on the LPGA Tour in years. Only 15 feet ... the gallery aware, aware of the pain and passion of Lopez's quest, was ready to explode in celebration ... . But the putt on the final hole ... missed, leaving Lopez a runner-up for the fourth time.[60]

Nancy Lopez, left, hugs British golfer Alison Nicholas after Nicholas beat Lopez in the U.S. Women's Open in North Plains, Oregon, in July 1997. Nicholas defeated Lopez by one stroke.

Lopez, despite her second-place finish, had played like a champion. She became the first golfer in women's history ever to shoot four rounds in the sixties in the event. She had rounds of sixty-nine, sixty-eight, sixty-nine, and sixty-nine. Lopez's score of nine under par tied her for the best-ever finish in the tournament, but she still only managed a second-place finish, one shot behind winner, Alison Nicholas. Vonders summarized: "She became the first player to shoot four US Women's Open rounds in the 60s, scored well enough to win all but one of the previous fifty-one Opens and still lost by one stroke."[61] D'Amato elaborated even further: "Lost isn't the right word. ... Not when you put the pressure on your opponent all day long and she responds, every time. Nancy Lopez didn't lose the Open to Alison Nicholas. She just didn't win it."[62]

In an interview after the match was over, Lopez, still fighting back tears, stated:

> It's a tough thing, because I've always wanted to win the US Open, and this was really, I felt, my time to do it. ... There's got to be a word between disappointed and happy. I'm not really disappointed because I thought I played the best I could. But, I'm not happy, because I didn't win... I probably won't sleep tonight, because I'll be thinking about every shot and what went on and what we did. And what I could have done.[63]

A Great Year

Her strong finish in the Open and her earlier win at the Chick-Fil-A tournament meant that Lopez finished 1997 in good standing. She climbed to ninth on the money list, her best finish in many years. And despite playing in only sixteen events, she had produced nine top-ten finishes. She also finished fifth on the tour in scoring average with 70.70 and was fourth in rounds under par at nine.

Prior to the start of the 1997 season, Lopez had seriously considered making that year the last of her career. But encouraged by how well she had played throughout the year, Lopez decided to go back out for another season. She told reporters that she was still

Lifetime Accomplishments

Nancy Lopez's list of accomplishments is a lengthy one. Victorious in forty-eight LPGA Tours, Lopez won three major tournaments: the LPGA Championship in 1978, 1985, and 1988. She is the only female golfer in history to earn Rookie of the Year, Player of the Year, and Vare Trophy honors in the same year, 1978. She repeated as Player of the Year three more times in 1979, 1985, and 1989. She also led the money list during three seasons: 1978, 1979, and 1985. In 2000 Lopez was named one of the LPGA's top fifty players and teachers during the LPGA's fiftieth anniversary celebration. She was praised for her outstanding contributions to the game. She remains the youngest player ever to be named to the LPGA Hall of Fame and is also a member of the World Golf Hall of Fame.

She is the first woman ever to receive the Francis Ouimet Award for Lifelong Contributions to Golf. In 2003 she was named to *Hispanic Business* magazine's list of 80 Elite Hispanic Women, and in 2007 she won a sports award for her work with the media. As of December 12, 2007, Lopez was seventh in all-time wins on the LPGA with her forty-eight victories. She is also one of only five women in golf who has earned more than one million dollars in a career. Her total career earnings, as of late 2007, are $5,301,391. She also holds the record for the most top-ten finishes in one year. In 1985 Lopez had twenty-one top tens.

During her long career, Lopez won forty-eight LPGA Tour victories and three major championships.

competitive and that she loved playing too much to quit. Her near miss at the U.S. Women's Open renewed Lopez's faith in her game. Her earlier victory and close finish encouraged her to hope for even better the following year.

Despite the resurgence in her golf skills, Lopez still struggled, however, with being away from home for long periods of time. Her daughters were reaching their teenage years and she felt she needed to be with them. "I think it's more difficult to balance the two (career and family) now than when my daughters were younger. I think they need mom around more than ever. There's more things to worry about as teenagers and that makes it more difficult for me to leave them."[64] Lopez would continue to place her family first but would return to the tour in 1998.

Balancing Act

"Balancing career and family is a continual challenge, and if Lopez errs, it's on the side of family and at the expense of her career."

—Sportswriter Gary D'Amato. Gary D'Amato, "In 20 Years, She's Won Everything There Is in Women's Golf Except the US Open," *Milwaukee Journal Sentinel*, June 28, 1998.

A Lackluster Year

After having such a good year in 1997, Lopez was sorely disappointed in her play during the following year. She continued to play a limited schedule but had difficulty even making the cut in tournaments. Players usually play two rounds of golf on Thursday and Friday and then the top sixty or seventy golfers get to play the weekend. Missing the cut means that someone has failed to score well enough to make that top group of golfers. Lopez failed to make the weekend a number of times in 1998.

Lopez, despite her lackluster performance, again entered the U.S. Women's Open in July 1998. She played poorly, shooting a seventy-seven on Thursday and an eight-three on Friday, well below the cut line. Her humor came through, however, as Brian Wicker reports: "A smiling Lopez marched down the 18th fairway [on Friday] with a white towel on the end of her putter, waving it in surrender."[65]

Knight was with her during the 1998 Open and watched her miss the cut. He walked with the fans who followed Lopez, but was able to spend a few moments with her between holes, generally holding her hand and offering words of encouragement. He said: "I just feel for her when she struggles. ... It's like you feel for your

Lopez's husband Ray Knight was with her during the 1998 U.S. Open, and tried to offer her words of encouragement and support after she missed the cut.

child, you just feel so hurt for her. It's not a matter of pressure, it's just of protectiveness because she's struggling so much. You just want to protect her."[66]

Despite her poor showing at the Open, Lopez told reporters that she was still just as competitive as ever, but she was concerned about her poor play. She realized that part of the problem was that during the time she spent at home with her family, she seldom practiced. She knew from experience that in order to win consistently, she needed to spend more time on the course and totally concentrate on her game. She was, however, reluctant to give up family time to do this.

Despite her poor play, Lopez was awarded the 1998 Bob Jones Award, the highest honor given by the United States Golf Association. Named after amateur superstar Bob Jones of the 1920s and 1930s, the award is given to recognize outstanding sportsmanship in golf.

Off and On the Course

With her golf game not up to her high standards, Lopez began to seriously consider retirement. She cut back her schedule even further and played in only a handful of tournaments in 1999, 2000, and 2001. Devoting the majority of her time to her family, Lopez also began to increase her commitments to several ventures outside of golf.

Lopez began volunteering her time to a number of charitable organizations. Her primary interest has been with Aid for the Handicapped, a group that helps those, especially children, with physical disabilities. Lopez has worked with a number of the children and has made a number of fundraising appearances. She says her work with this organization has helped not only fill her idle hours but has also helped fulfill her life.

Lopez also began to devote much of her time and effort to educating women golfers about the equipment they use. She started her own company, NancyLopezGolf in 1997 in order to provide women with good golf equipment. She stated: "Women can and will enjoy golf more when they have the right clubs in their hands. They need to know that they no longer have to be content to adjust their game to men's clubs."[67]

Nancy Lopez (right) appears with Dinah Shore in 1984. Lopez has always played in charity tournaments and enjoys working with young golfers.

Lopez also was elected to the board of directors of Women's Golf Unlimited, the parent company of her own organization. Doug Buffinton, the president of Women's Golf Unlimited, stated:

> She is the perfect spokeswoman for proper club-fitting. As more and more women take up the game or decide to get more serious about it, they have as their advocate Nancy Lopez, one of the most successful golfers of all times. She knows what she's talking about and golfers listen when she offers counsel.[68]

In addition to these commitments, Lopez remained active on the golf course, playing in many charity tournaments. In May 2001 she played in the second annual Celebrity Professional-Amateur at the Seven Springs Mountain Resort in Champion, Pennsylvania. The proceeds from the event benefited breast cancer research. Lopez also spent several hours at the women's and junior's clinic at the event. She later reported that she especially enjoyed teaching young and aspiring golfers.

Being especially aware of the hardships that many of the Mexican Americans face in her hometown community of Roswell, New Mexico, Lopez has committed her time and money to helping needy citizens there. Her importance to that community was revealed when the Roswell School Board changed the name of her old elementary school, Flora Vista, to Nancy Lopez Elementary School. She remains a strong role model for the Hispanic youth of New Mexico and elsewhere.

Chapter 5

Retirement or Not?

After several years of poor play on the tour, Nancy Lopez announced in March 2002 that she was retiring and would no longer play full time on the LPGA Tour. She was forty-five years old and hadn't had a victory in five years. According to sports reporter Lisette Hilton, Lopez told her that "she didn't want to be one of those athletes that would keep playing even though she couldn't perform on a high level anymore."[69] Lopez announced that the year 2002 would be her last full season and that, in the future, she would play in only three to five tournaments a year, thus allowing her to spend even more time with her family.

In part, this decision to retire was due to her fall to 157th on the money list in 2001, and because she had not made a cut in some time. Lopez had always insisted that when the time came that she could not play competitively, she would retire and spend more quality time with her children.

Earlier that same year, Lopez received a blow that affected her deeply and took away some of the joy she had always felt

A young Nancy Lopez (right) stands with her parents, Marina and Domingo Lopez. The death of her father in 2001 re-enforced her decision to retire and spend more time with her family.

playing golf. Her father, the man who had been with her from the beginning and who had encouraged her to play, died in April from heart failure. While his death was not unexpected, the loss, nonetheless, was a heavy blow to Lopez and helped reenforce her decision to retire and spend more time with her family.

A Last Open

Several months after her father's death, Lopez entered her last U.S. Women's Open. Sportswriter Chuck Schoffner described what happened: "With a tip of her visor and a bow to the crowd, Nancy Lopez closed out another chapter in a remarkable career. Cheers rang in her ears and tears welled in her eyes … as Lopez played for the twenty-fifth and final time in the US Women's Open."[70] The date was July 5, 2002, and Lopez's second-round score of seventy-nine left her with a score of twenty over par for the first two rounds of the tournament. Her score was well below the cut line, meaning she would fail to play the final two days of the event.

She did not do well in her two rounds on Thursday and Friday but she did have her usual moments of brilliance. Overall, however, her play was well below her usual standards. She thrilled the fans, though, by joking with them. On one hole, after she had putted out, she gave the ball to a fan, telling him: "Hey would you want this ball? It doesn't want to go in for me."[71]

The fact that she missed the cut did not seem to matter to the thousands of fans who had turned out to see Lopez once again try to win the elusive Open. The gallery erupted into cheers whenever Lopez holed a putt or hit a good drive. The applause could be heard throughout the course. Schoffner described the adoration: "And applaud they did—from the bleachers, from the hillsides, from the luxury suites, and along the fairway. ... The cheers reached a crescendo as Lopez walked up the eighteenth fairway. You would have thought she was winning the Open instead of leaving it."[72]

Lopez was tearful as she described her feelings about the loyalty of her fans, admitting that there was nothing better than walking up the eighteenth fairway at the end of a match and hearing the cheering. After playing the last hole, she smiled as she faced the crowd and then tipped her hat to them. The fans, members of Nancy's Navy, erupted once again into cheers and yells as she left the course. "They adored her," sportswriter Joe Posnanski wrote. "This wasn't just admiration for twenty-five years of good golf. No, they loved her. They stood. They cheered. They stood again. They cheered again."[73]

Later, Lopez commented on her last U.S. Open: "I just feel real fortunate. There's nothing for me to get mad about. Yes, I am frustrated out there, but I've been able to do something that I love. So the frustration—I just kind of ignore it." She then stated that her husband had told her to just enjoy herself and do her best. "But my best to me is, you know, in the top ten. I don't like just playing to miss cuts."[74]

The End of 2002

Throughout her final year on the tour, Lopez was swarmed by both the media and fans. During 2002, the galleries that followed her were just as large as they were during her heyday and far larger than those that followed other players.

In September 2002 Lopez played in her last professional tournament. Once again she walked off the course to cheers and words of appreciation. Lopez shed a lot of tears on her farewell tour in 2002. Repeatedly, however, she said it was time for her to retire. She admitted that it was difficult to leave: "The farewell tour has been a sad tour for me, because I've had to say goodbye to a lot of people I probably won't see for a while."[75]

Back in Full Swing

After retirement in 2002, Nancy Lopez and her husband Ray Knight devoted much of their time advocating heart health. Their decision was based primarily on Lopez's family history of heart disease as well as Knight's own heart trouble. Working with pharmaceutical company GlaxoSmithKline, the couple embarked on a multicity tour they called "Back in Full Swing." The tour's purpose was to help people and their families return to healthy living after a heart attack. During the tour, the couple talked of how they worked together as a family to be heart healthy.

Lopez and Knight shared their own stories as part of the presentations. Knight: "I always thought of myself as bullet proof because of my generally healthy lifestyle and athletic career. When I found out I had suffered a heart attack, I was scared, concerned, anxious, and upset. . . . [Now] I have a new sense of hope and optimism about my life." He credited his wife and family, along with his doctors, for helping him return to a healthy lifestyle.

Lopez recounted her own history: "After witnessing both my parents suffer from heart disease and my father die from heart failure, you can imagine how incredibly frightened I was when we learned that Ray had suffered a heart attack. The thought of losing Ray was unbearable, so we work together to make sure he lives a long, healthy life."

PR Newswire, "Sports Icons Visit Chicago to Help Residents Get Back in Full Swing After a Heart Attack," PR Newswire, August 18, 2004.

Nancy Lopez applauds as Se Ri Pak (right) holds her Hall of fame trophy Lopez is considered an ambassador for women's golf.

One reporter wrote: "Nancy Lopez has spent twenty-five years on this ride, celebrating victories and lamenting losses, and now, she's in that final turn. There she was ... smiling one moment and crying the next as she addressed reporters."[76]

Accolades Pour In

As Lopez finished her amazing career, her peers and the press began to comment on what Lopez had meant to women's golf. Superstar Annika Sorenstam told reporters that while growing up in Sweden, she had always dreamed of playing golf as well as Lopez. She said: "It's so sad to see her saying good-bye. But she's doing it in style. Which is her whole career. I think we're all very thankful for what she's done."[77]

What may be most sorely missed is Lopez as an ambassador for women's golf. Australian golf star Karrie Webb commented: "I think it would take a few of us out here with the younger players just to fill those shoes and do some of the similar things she did as just one person."[78] Webb added: "She's one of the tour's most approachable people, someone willing to help younger golfers and promote the game. She does it through interviews, through promotions, through simply being a good ambassador."[79]

Solheim Cup Captain

During the next two years, Lopez played in a few tournaments, finishing well out of the money. She spent the majority of her time with her family and doing volunteer and charity work for a variety of enterprises. In January 2004, however, Nancy Lopez's name was back in the news when she was named the unanimous

Captain Nancy Lopez is surrounded by her victorious U.S. team after winning the 2005 Solheim Cup.

choice to captain the U.S. women's team in the 2005 Solheim Cup matches. LPGA commissioner Ty Votaw said, "There could be no better ambassador of the talent, heart, and enthusiasm of the event."[80]

The Solheim Cup, first played in 1990, pits the best women golfers in America against the best women golfers in Europe. It is similar in format to the Ryder's Cup, the men's event played every two years. The event features match play instead of stroke play, meaning that a team of two American players are pitted against a European twosome and the scoring is done hole by hole, rather than after eighteen holes.

Lopez, whose only Solheim Cup appearance was as a player on the initial victorious 1990 American team, told reporters that she was thrilled to be selected. She went on to say: "I'm psyched to get out there and support them, because I know we can get that cup back."[81] She later added: "It's an honor that I don't think you can really describe … it's the top feather in my cap."[82]

Europe had defeated the American team in the 2003 Cup so Lopez's team was looking forward to playing the 2005 event on American soil at Crooked Stick Golf Course in Carmel, Indiana. The United States was successful in regaining the Cup during the matches at Crooked Stick, winning 15 ½ to 12 ½.

Considering a Comeback

Captaining the Solheim team rekindled Lopez's interest in a more active playing schedule. In early 2006 Lopez joined the Legends Tour to play in the June Hy-Vee Classic. The Legends Tour, still in its infancy as far as professional sports is concerned, was created in 1999 for women golfers over the age of forty-five. It was the women's answer to the men's Champion Tour, a very popular and lucrative venture for male golfers over the age of fifty. Players such as Lee Trevino, Hale Irwin, Gary Player, and others had found the Champions Tour to be a good place to continue their competitive golf. Jane Blalock, president of the Legends Tour, told reporters that she hoped the new tour would attract some of the best women golfers in the world. "We're the pioneers of women's golf," she stated, "and this is our tour."[83]

Paula Creamer hits a shot while Nancy Lopez watches during the final day of practice for the 2007 McDonald's LPGA Championship. In making her comeback, Lopez wondered how she would do against the game's current players.

Lopez finished in a tie for twenty-ninth place. Despite her relatively poor showing, however, Lopez indicated that she would like to play in more events in the future. But she had other ideas as well.

After the Legends event, she began to seriously consider making a comeback on the regular tour. "Watching Paula (Creamer) and Natalie (Gulbis) and all the young players [during the Solheim competition] hit the ball, I would sit there and say, 'I remember when I hit it just like that.' It just motivated me to think maybe I can do it one more time."[84]

Once again, however, her biggest obstacle was her weight and energy level.   Reporter Chris Silva elaborated: "The Doritos got the best of Nancy Lopez. Those, and all the other junk food she consumed. … Her blood pressure was rising. … Her cholesterol was up. … So Lopez … paid a visit to her doctor."[85]

The physician suggested diet and exercise. During the next month, Lopez lost 10 pounds (5kg) and began another exercise program. Three months later, she had shed 28 pounds (13kg) and found that her chronically painful feet and knees had stopped hurting.

It was at this time that she began to nurse the hope of a comeback. She agreed to play in the Jamie Farr Owens Corning Classic in Toledo, Ohio, in the fall of 2006, making this her first event on the regular tour in over a year. Although she did not make the cut, she felt somewhat encouraged about her play. She reluctantly admitted: "I'm not going to hit 260 yards [drives] anymore. Maybe once in awhile, I might. But I've got to accept what I can do now, and I really haven't done well with that in the past few years."[86]

She told reporters that she was still working on her game, practicing her drives, and trying to improve her putting. She began to put in the hours on the driving range that she had earlier in her career. She also told the media that she was curious about how she would do against the current game's best players. "I really hadn't picked up a club in awhile," she said. "But I enjoy being back out and competing. I'm going to try and play a little bit more and get a lot of the rust out and see what I can do."[87]

On the Tour Again

After hours of practice and the loss of nearly 40 pounds, (18kg) Lopez felt she was ready to compete again. And yet, at age fifty, she knew she faced many difficulties. Despite this, she was

Despite missing three tournament cuts through June 2007, the crowds following Lopez were as big as ever, proving her enduring popularity with golf fans.

cautiously optimistic. She told reporters that her mental game was still as tough as ever and that she also felt good physically. She hoped for a quick top-ten finish.

Others, including most golf analysts were not as optimistic. One expert elaborated: "She's fifty now, more than twice the age of many young standouts on the LPGA Tour."[88] Another analyst pointed out that of the last seventy-two events she'd played in, Lopez had only finished in the top ten once.

Lopez's first event on her comeback attempt was the 2007 Ginn Open. Unfortunately, Lopez fell well short of making the two-day cut with rounds of eighty-three and eighty. She finished last in the 140-player field, but she did have moments of the old brilliance, birdieing three of the final five holes. "I wanted to play better than I did, for sure. I'm disappointed with the numbers, but getting out here and playing is the only way you can come back."[89]

Playing with a broken toe may have hurt her chances to do well. She had broken it the previous week when she had inadvertently walked into a piece of iron furniture. "My feet are killing me. The toe didn't bother me when I swung at all. It was just walking. I got tired of limping on it."[90] As she finished the second round, she announced that she was going to continue to work on her game and would hopefully do better in the next tournament she chose to enter.

Many analysts criticized her decision, pointing out that Lopez was no longer the competitive golfer she once was. Other writers supported her decision wholeheartedly. "In the case of golfers, the temptation to compete when no longer competitive is seriously seductive," Ron Sirak wrote. "And when it comes to a player of the stature of Nancy Lopez ... they should be given free rein to entertain the fans and enjoy themselves to their heart's desire."[91]

Crowd Appeal

"Much like Arnold Palmer, even as her performance faded, fans still find her relevant."

—LPGA commissioner Ty Votaw. Andrew Seligman, "Finishing Swing: With Two LPGA Events Left, Nancy Lopez Takes Time to Reflect on Her Career," *Columbian*, September 13, 2002.

Sirak went on to point out that superstar Arnold Palmer played on the PGA Tour in some of the major tournaments until he was seventy-five despite shooting rounds in the eighties. "Lopez is every bit in Palmer's mold—both love the game—as well as the fame. They thrive on the adoration and feel by continuing to play

Home Life

Home for Nancy Lopez is in Albany, Georgia, where she lives with her family on a 600-acre (243-hectare) farm. Lopez loves to cook and enjoys hunting and fishing. She says the best thing about hunting is "just being out in the woods, seeing the morning open up and the animals come out."[1]

Lopez and her husband have three daughters: Ashley Marie, Erinn Shea, and Torri Heather. Lopez has always been a good mother, making her children her first priority. Writer Alice Steinbach elaborates: "Watching her with her daughters, she is a warm, affectionate, no-nonsense mother—and listening to her talk about her priorities—children, husband, home, and golf, in that order —it isn't impossible to accept the idea that there are more important things in the lives of Lopez and Knight than money."[2]

Her marriage to Ray Knight is very traditional, Lopez says. He is the head of the household, and Lopez fulfills

Family has always been very important to Nancy Lopez.

the same role her own mother did. "I do it all," Lopez once said. "I cook, I clean, I wash dishes, I wash clothes. . . . I love being at home with the kids. They're stable."[3]

1. Quoted in "Nancy Lopez Biography," BookRags Web site. www.bookrags.com/biography/nancy-lopez-sports.
2. Alice Steinbach, "Nancy Lopez Knight: Golfer Extraordinaire, Mother, Wife Ordinaire," *Chicago-Sun Times*, May 17, 1987.
3. Quoted in Sally Jenkins, "Making Marriage, Golf Work," *Chicago-Sun Times*, June 28, 1987.

they are paying back a game that has paid them well. Lopez hasn't won … in ten years. … So what? If she wants to play, she has earned the right."[92]

Through June 2007, Lopez played in three tournaments, but failed to make the cut in any of them. Despite her lackluster scoring, the crowds following her were as big as ever. And her smile never wavered.

Legacy

Despite her poor play in later years, nothing can diminish the legacy that Lopez has left to the golf world. Writing in 1998, Gary D'Amato elaborated:

> Lopez has won 48 tournaments, three LPGA Championships, more than five million in prize money and the undying loyalty of millions of fans. She is one of the fourteen members of the LPGA Hall of Fame and the only one, it should be noted, who got there while raising a family. She is an American icon.[93]

One of the strongest legacies she is leaving is her immense crowd appeal. Regardless of how busy she was or where she stood on the leaderboard, Lopez never failed to give autographs, pose for pictures with fans, or shake hands. Brian Wicker elaborates: "Lopez attracts fans who would much rather watch her miss the cut than nearly anyone else win the tournament. ... Lopez gave the women's game a transcendent folk heroine. Her combination of skill and style endeared her to fans."[94] Said Jennifer McCormack, a long time fan: "It's just a pleasure to watch her play. To me she makes golf what it is."[95]

An Icon of Women's Golf

"When you think of women's golf, you think of Nancy."

—Golf superstar Annika Sorenstam. Anne M. Peterson, "Nancy Lopez Says More Goodbyes." *AP Online*, September 13, 2002.

Sports analysts throughout the country, along with many of Lopez's peers and fellow competitors agree that Lopez will be remembered as a golf pioneer and champion. Golf star Juli Inkster states: "She brings a certain charisma and leadership to our tour. She's been great to this tour. She's given her heart and soul to this tour."[96] Inkster went on to say: "It was not just about her golf. She's got charisma, and she has been able, at times, to carry the whole tour. She has always had the personality and the

Morgan Pressel was the winner of the Nancy Lopez Award in 2006, which is an award given to the world's best female amateur golfer.

smile. Not too many people can do what she has done, and she is so very gracious. She is an awesome player."[97]

Young and up-and-coming player Morgan Pressel adds her opinion: "I certainly look up to her. She's a wonderful competitor and a great player and a great person, and I think that's characteristic of Nancy Lopez. And the way she interacted with the fans and the media and everything, along with her golf game, are things that I try to emulate every day."[98] Pressel was the 2006 winner of the Nancy Lopez Award, an award given to the world's best female amateur golfer. The purpose of the award is not only to recognize the best players in women's golf but to increase the public's awareness of women's amateur golf in general.

Many sports analysts also report that while the sports world is full of superstars who flaunt their success and popularity, Lopez never did. She never lost sight that she came from humble beginnings, and she always credited her parents with her determination to succeed. She never failed to give fans her attention. She remained throughout her career approachable and friendly. She just kept smiling and being herself—to the delight of the golf world and her fans. Her father had taught her to "play happy." Through all of her success, Lopez continued to do just that—she played happy—and surrounded everyone with her warmth and charisma.

Her Lasting Impact

"Nancy's one of a kind. We won't see many more people in the history of the LPGA have the impact she did."

—Golf star Karrie Webb. Len Ziehm, "Walking up the 18th, Nancy Lopez Nears the End of an Illustrious Career," *Chicago-Sun Times*, May 31, 2002.

Nancy Lopez dominated women's golf for nearly two decades. She also became one of the most popular stars in sports. She did it by being herself. Until 2002, she was the only female golfer ever to have her picture on the cover of *Sports Illustrated*. Writer Joe Posnanski describes the significance of her 1978 appearance on the magazine cover: "That shows you how hard it is for a woman golfer to break through into America's consciousness.

But now, even people who know nothing about women's golf know Lopez. She has inspired millions."[99]

"She was Tiger Woods once, storming the Tour, invincible and unprecedented," writer Lew Price summarizes. "She had the game, but she had a smile, too, and a grace seldom seen. She became a hero at a time when women weren't accorded much hero worship in sports. … Her swing was smooth and powerful, but it was her personality and feminism that drew new fans to the women's game."[100]

When asked how she wanted to be remembered, Lopez once answered:

> I want them to remember a great player, a person that was aggressive and competitive, who always smiled no matter what, and that I was always a giving person, to my fans, to whomever I came in contact with. I want to be remembered as one of the great players and one of the friendliest.[101]

There is no doubt that Lopez will be remembered in just that way.

Notes

Introduction: LPGA Superstar

1. Len Ziehm, "Walking up the 18th, Nancy Lopez Nears the End of an Illustrious Career." *Chicago Sun-Times*, May 31, 2002.
2. Latino Legends in Sports, "Nancy Lopez," LatinoSportsLegends.com, www.latinosportslegends.com/Lopez_Nancy-bio.htm.
3. Quoted in Lisette Hilton, "Lopez Is LPGA's Knight in Shining Armor," ESPN.com, http://espn.go.com/classic/biography/s/Lopez_Nancy.html.
4. Ron Sirak, "The Lopez Legacy," *Columbian*, May 6, 1998.
5. Dick Wimmer, *The Women's Game: Great Champions in Women's Sports*. Short Hills, NJ: Burford, 2000, p. 67.
6. Paul Harber, "Lopez's Feats as an LPGA Rookie a Tough Act for Woods to Follow," *Denver Rocky Mountain News*, April 6, 1997.
7. Eric Olson, "Lopez Returning to Tour at 50," *Cincinnati Post*, March 7, 2007.

Chapter 1: A Golfing Prodigy

8. Nancy Lopez with Peter Schwed, *The Education of a Woman Golfer*. New York: *Simon* and Schuster, 1979, p. 9.
9. Wimmer, *The Women's Game*, p. 65.
10. Lopez with Schwed, *The Education of a Woman Golfer*, p. 18.
11. Donna Adams, "The Inspirational Nancy Lopez," in *Chicken Soup for the Woman Golfer's Soul*, by Jack Canfield et al. Deerfield Beach, FL: Health Communications, 2007, p. 146.
12. Lopez with Schwed, *The Education of a Woman Golfer*, p. 24.
13. Lopez with Schwed, *The Education of a Woman Golfer*, p. 23.
14. Lopez with Schwed, *The Education of a Woman Golfer*, p. 23.
15. Nancy Lopez and Don Wade, *The Complete Golfer*. Chicago, IL: Contemporarys, 1987, p. 195.

16. Quoted in Lopez with Schwed, *The Education of a Woman Golfer*, p. 23.
17. Lopez with Schwed, *The Education of a Woman Golfer*, p. 73.
18. Lopez with Schwed, *The Education of a Woman Golfer*, p. 154.
19. Lopez and Wade, *The Complete Golfer*, p. 207.

Chapter 2: Rookie of the Year
20. History of Women's Golf in America, "From Amateur to Professional," History of Women's Golf in America Web site, www.historywomensgolfam.com/professional.htm.
21. Lopez with Schwed, *The Education of a Woman Golfer*, p. 130.
22. Lopez with Schwed, *The Education of a Woman Golfer*, p. 134.
23. Lopez with Schwed, *The Education of a Woman Golfer*, p. 138.
24. Lopez with Schwed, *The Education of a Woman Golfer*, p. 138.
25. Quoted in Sirak, "The Lopez Legacy."
26. Quoted in Brian Wicker, "Queen of the LPGA," *Star Tribune* (Minneapolis, MN), August 16, 1998.
27. Doug Ferguson, "Lopez Once was Tiger of Tour Twenty Years Ago, She Dominated LPGA Field," *Denver Rocky Mountain News*, May 10, 1998.
28. Quoted in Harber, "Lopez's Feats as an LPGA Rookie."
29. Quoted in Randall Mell, "Fond Farewell for Nancy Lopez," *South Florida Sun-Sentinel*, July 2, 2002.
30. Quoted in Joe Posnanski, "Nancy Lopez Touched Many," *Knight Ridder/Tribune News Service*, July 5, 2002.
31. Lopez with Schwed, *The Education of a Woman Golfer*, p. 146.
32. Bob Lutz, "Nancy Lopez Leaves Golf with Ultimate Grace," *Knight Ridder/Tribune News Service*, July 5, 2002.
33. Alice Steinbach, "Nancy Lopez Knight: Golfer Extraordinaire, Mother, Wife Ordinaire," *Chicago-Sun Times*, May 17, 1987.
34. Mell, "Fond Farewell for Nancy Lopez."
35. Lopez with Schwed, *The Education of a Woman Golfer*, p. 160.
36. Quoted in Ferguson, "Lopez Once Was Tiger of Tour."

Chapter 3: Balancing Family and Career
37. Lopez with Schwed, *The Education of a Woman Golfer*, p. 184.

38. Lopez with Schwed, *The Education of a Woman Golfer*, p. 187.
39. Steinbach, "Nancy Lopez Knight."
40. Quoted in Steinbach, "Nancy Lopez Knight."
41. Quoted in "Nancy Lopez Biography," BookRags Web site, www.bookrags.com/Nancy_Lopez.
42. Quoted in Steinbach, "Nancy Lopez Knight."
43. Quoted in "Nancy Lopez Biography."
44. Quoted in Sally Jenkins, "Making Marriage, Golf Work," *Chicago Sun-Times*, June 28, 1987.
45. Jenkins, "Making Marriage, Golf Work."
46. Quoted in Jenkins, "Making Marriage, Golf Work."
47. Quoted in Latino Legends in Sports, "Nancy Lopez."
48. Lopez and Wade, *The Complete Golfer*, p. ix.
49. Lopez and Wade, *The Complete Golfer*, p. viii, 201.
50. Lopez and Wade, *The Complete Golfer*, p. x.

Chapter 4: Struggling to Find Her Game

51. Quoted in "Nancy Lopez Biography."
52. Quoted in "Nancy Lopez Biography."
53. Bob Harig, "Back in the Swing," *Denver Rocky Mountain News*, May 11, 1997.
54. Quoted in Harig, "Back in the Swing."
55. Quoted in Harig, "Back in the Swing."
56. Gary D'Amato, "In 20 Years, She's Won Everything There Is in Women's Golf except the US Open," *Milwaukee Journal Sentinel*, June 28, 1998.
57. Quoted in "Nancy Lopez Biography."
58. Jason Vonders, "Nancy Lopez: She's Anything but a Loser," *Columbian*, July 15, 1997.
59. Quoted in Wicker, "Queen of the LPGA."
60. Lew Price, "Still on Fire After All These Years," *Denver Rocky Mountain News*, March 29, 1998.
61. Vonders, "Nancy Lopez: She's Anything but a Loser."
62. D'Amato, "In 20 Years, She's Won Everything."
63. Quoted in "Only Tears for Nancy," *Cincinnati Post*, July 14, 1997.
64. Quoted in Price, "Still on Fire After All These Years."
65. Wicker, "Queen of the LPGA."

66. Quoted in Jenkins, "Making Marriage, Golf Work."
67. Quoted in "Nancy Lopez Sets Her Sights on Educating Women about Good Equipment Decisions," *Business Wire*, February 22, 2003.
68. Quoted in "Nancy Lopez Sets Her Sights on Educating Women about Good Equipment Decisions."

Chapter 5: Retirement or Not?
69. Hilton, "Lopez Is LPGA's Knight in Shining Armor."
70. Chuck Schoffner, "Lopez Plays Final U.S. Women's Open," *AP Online*, July 5, 2002.
71. Quoted in Schoffner, "Lopez Plays Final U.S. Women's Open."
72. Schoffner, "Lopez Plays Final U.S. Women's Open."
73. Posnanski, "Nancy Lopez Touched Many."
74. Quoted in Lutz, "Nancy Lopez Leaves Golf with Ultimate Grace."
75. Quoted in Anne M. Peterson, "Nancy Lopez Says More Goodbyes." *AP Online*, September 13, 2002.
76. Mell, "Fond Farewell for Nancy Lopez."
77. Quoted in Posnanski, "Nancy Lopez Touched Many."
78. Quoted in Peterson, "Nancy Lopez Says More Goodbyes."
79. Quoted in Andrew Seligman, "Finishing Swing: With Two LPGA Events Left, Nancy Lopez Takes Time to Reflect on her Career," *Columbian*, September 13, 2002.
80. Quoted in "Nancy Lopez Named Solheim Cup Captain," *AP Online*, January 26, 2004.
81. Quoted in "Nancy Lopez Named Solheim Cup Captain."
82. Quoted in "Q and A with Nancy Lopez," LPGA.com, www.lpga.com/content_1.aspx?pid=4563&mid=1.
83. Quoted in ESPN. com, "Four Events, $1.4 Million Prize Money on Legends Tour," ESPN. com, March 28, 2006. http://sports.espn.go.com/print?id=2387358&type=story.
84. Quoted in Olson, "Lopez Returning to Tour at 50."
85. Chris Silva, "Slimmer Lopez to Tee Up," *Detroit Free Press*, July 13, 2006.
86. Quoted in Silva, "Slimmer Lopez to Tee Up."
87. Quoted in Sports Illustrated.com, "Lopez Shooting for Return to Tour," Sports Illustrated.com, June 23, 2006.

http://sportsillustrated.com/2006/golf/06/23/lopez.hyvee.

88. Quoted in Golf.com, "Lopez Starting a Comeback on the LPGA Tour," Golf.com, April 12, 2007. www.golf.com/golf/tours_news/article/0,28136,1609522,00.html.

89. Quoted in Golf.com, "Lopez Comeback Starts with Last Place Finish," Golf.com, April 13, 2007. www.golf.com/golf/tours_news/article/0,28136,1610525,00.htm.

90. Quoted in Golf.com, "Lopez Comeback Starts with Last Place Finish."

91. Ron Sirak, "Lopez Falls Victim to Golf's Linger Factor," ESPN.com, April 25, 2007. http://sports.espn.go.com/golf/columns/story?columnist=sirak_ron&id=2849085.

92. Sirak, "Lopez Falls Victim to Golf's Linger Factor."

93. D'Amato, "In 20 Years, She's Won Everything."

94. Wicker, "Queen of the LPGA."

95. Quoted in Wimmer, *The Women's Game*, p. 66.

96. Quoted in Seligman, "Finishing Swing."

97. Quoted in Mell, "Fond Farewell for Nancy Lopez."

98. Quoted in Golf.com, "Lopez Starting a Comeback on the LPGA Tour."

99. Posnanski, "Nancy Lopez Touched Many."

100. Price, "Still on Fire After All These Years."

101. Quoted in Mell, "Fond Farewell for Nancy Lopez."

Important Dates

January 6, 1957
Nancy Marie Lopez was born in Roswell, New Mexico.

1965
Played her first golf at the age of eight.

1966
Won her first tournament at the age of nine.

1973
Named number-one amateur in the United States.

1977
Dropped out of college to turn professional.

1978
During rookie year on tour, won five tournaments in a row; for the year, she won a total of nine.

1979
Won eight tournaments after a January wedding to sportscaster Tim Melton.

October 1982
Married professional baseball player Ray Knight.

1983
Birth of first daughter Ashley. Followed by two other daughters in 1986 and 1991.

1985
Led the money list and received Player of the Year honors.

1987
Youngest female golfer to be inducted into LPGA Hall of Fame.

April 1997
Forty-eighth victory at the Chick Fil-A Tournament.

March 2002
Announced retirement.

2005
Captained the U.S. team in the Solheim Cup.

2007
Comeback on Tour unsuccessful.

For More Information

Books

Judy L. Hasday, *Extraordinary Women Athletes*. Chicago: Children's Press, 2000. This book focuses on exception female athletes and includes a section on Lopez.

Nancy Robinson, *Nancy Lopez: Wonder Woman of Golf*. Chicago: Children's Press, 1979. A biography of Lopez, covering her childhood and rookie year on the LPGA Tour.

Periodicals

AP Online, "Knight Tries to Console His Wife, Nancy Lopez," *AP Online*, July 3, 1998.

Tom Canavan, "Nancy Lopez Considering a Career in the Broadcast Booth," *AP Worldstream*, June 29, 2002.

Mel Reisner, "Nancy Lopez Retiring after 25 Years," *AP Online*, March 13, 2002.

Ron Sirak, "Nancy Lopez: A Smile That Lasted 20 Years," *AP Online*, May 5, 1998.

Newpapers

Reid Hutchins, "Nancy Lopez to Retire from Women's Golf Tour," *Daily Journal of Commerce* (Portland, Oregon), July 30, 2002.

Bob Lutz, "Nancy Lopez Leaves Golf with Ultimate Grace," *Knight Ridder/Tribune News Service*, July 5, 2002.

Newswire

PR Newswire, "Celebrity Pro-Am Features Professional Lady Golfers: Nancy Lopez to Attend," *PR Newswire*, May 16, 2001.

Internet Sources

CBS SportsLine.com, "Lopez, 50, Starting a Comeback Try

on LPGA Tour," CBS SportsLine.com, April 12, 2007.
www.sportsline.com/golf/story.10122211.

ESPN.com, "Lopez to Play First LPGA Event in over a Year,"
ESPN.com, July 6, 2006. http://sports.espn.go.com/golf/news/
story?id=2511064&campaign=rss&source=GOLFHeadlines.

Essortment, "Nancy Lopez Biography," Essortment.
http://nh.essortment.com/nancylopezbiog_rego.htm.

Golf Europe, "Nancy Lopez," Golf Europe.
www.golfeurope.com/almanac/players/lopez.htm.

LPGA.com, "Nancy Lopez: US Solheim Cup Team Captain,"
LPGA.com. www.lpga.com/content_1.aspx?pid=4573&mid=1.

Web Sites

ESPN.com (www.espn.com). A general sports Web site that
provides information on a variety of sports.

Ladies Professional Golf Association (www.lpga.com). A
Web site dedicated to women's golf.

Sports Illustrated (www.sportsillustrated.cnn.com). A Web site
that provides information and articles on a variety of sports.

Index

Picture Credits

About the Author

Anne Wallace Sharp is the author of the adult book *Gifts*, a compilation of stories about hospice patients; several children's books, including *Daring Pirate Women*; and thirteen other Lucent books. She has also written numerous magazine articles for both adults and juveniles. A retired registered nurse, Sharp has a degree in history. Her interests include reading, traveling, and spending time with her two grandchildren, Jacob and Nicole. Sharp lives in Beavercreek, Ohio.